Writing for Academic Publication

A Guide to Getting Started

Frank Parker
Louisiana State University

Kathryn Riley
University of Minnesota, Duluth

Parlay Press
Superior, Wisconsin

Parlay Press
P.O. Box 894
Superior, WI 54880
Telephone/Fax (218) 834-2508

Copyright © 1995 by Parlay Enterprises. All rights, including that of translation, reserved. No part of this document may be reproduced, stored in a retrieval system, or transmitted in any form or by any means, electronic, mechanical, recording, or otherwise, without the prior written permission of the publisher.

Frank Parker and Kathryn Riley

    Writing for academic publication
    ISBN 0-9644636-1-X

Contents

Acknowledgement v

Chapter 1   Introduction 1

Chapter 2   The Book Review 8
             Textbooks 9
             Collections 15

Chapter 3   Time Management 24
             Stage I: Random Reading 25
             Stage II: Focussed Reading 27
             Stage III: First Draft 31
             Stage IV: Final Draft 32
             An Overview 35

Chapter 4   The Abstract 37
             The Call for Papers 37
             Preparing the Abstract 41

Chapter 5   The Conference Presentation 50
             The Role of Conference Papers . . . 50
             Preparing an Effective
                    Conference Paper 52

Contents

Chapter 6	The Response Article	65
	Organization	66
	Tone	68
Chapter 7	The Research Article	72
	The Role of the Research Article	72
	Organization	74
	Length	80
Chapter 8	Introductions	84
Chapter 9	Examples	90
Chapter 10	Quotations	101
Chapter 11	Figures	107
Chapter 12	Metalanguage	117
Chapter 13	Conclusions	121
Chapter 14	Submitting Manuscripts for Publication	128
	Selecting a Journal	128
	Sending in the Manuscript	130
	The Review Process	135
Chapter 15	Conclusion	149
References		151

Acknowledgement

We want to thank Kim Campbell of the Air Force Institute of Technology for reading and commenting on the manuscript for this book and especially for trying it out in her classes.

Chapter 1: Introduction

Graduate students, assistant professors, and others contemplating or beginning an academic career face a dilemma.

On the one hand, WRITING IS DIFFICULT AND PEOPLE DREAD IT.

Many university faculty members avoid writing at all costs. Consider the panic with which many assistant professors face their fifth-year tenure review. They leave graduate school with no substantial publications; they rationalize not writing after graduate school (new courses to teach, meetings to attend); they force themselves into a flurry of writing activity during the tenure review; and, finally, they succumb to the inertia induced by a positive tenure decision or the bitterness generated by a negative one.

It's not just assistant professors who dread writing. A few years ago we were visiting a phonetician and journal editor in England. He told us of an American colleague--a full professor from a research university--who had spent the preceding year working at the phonetician's lab. He said, "I kept encouraging Professor _____ to write something for the journal. He had lots of energy; he would spend days in the lab running and cataloguing data, but he never was able to write anything--he had difficulty writing."

Even professional writers look upon the process with mixed feelings. A few years ago, Norman Mailer was being

Chapter 1: Introduction

interviewed by Bryant Gumbel on *Today*. Gumbel remarked that Mailer must enjoy writing. The author was indignant; his response ran something like this: "I hate writing; it's hard work. I enjoy *having written*, but I don't like writing."

On the other hand, ACADEMIC SUCCESS IN MOST FIELDS DEPENDS ON WRITING AND PUBLICATION.

One of the most persuasive cases for being able to write publishable papers has been made by the scientist Robert Day. He states that

> there is no question but that the goal of scientific research is publication. Scientists, starting as graduate students, are measured primarily not by their dexterity in laboratory manipulation, not by their innate knowledge of either broad or narrow scientific subjects, and certainly not by their wit or charm; they are measured, and become known (or remain unknown), by their *publications*. (1983: ix)

Indeed, this fact is often evident even to those just beginning academic careers. A graduate student in literature recently commented on this issue in the newsletter of the Modern Language Association, from an insightful first-hand perspective that we feel is worth quoting at length:

> Departments that do not have a job officer or a class (or set of classes) to provide instruction or guidance in cover-letter writing, c[urriculum] v[ita] preparation, reference hunting, article and manuscript preparation, grant writing, conference participation, job hunting outside academia, and so on are simply not doing the work an academic department should be doing in today's job market. To be blunt, academic departments, especially in the humanities, shirk their duties by instructing students on academic subjects alone.

Chapter 1: Introduction

> I suspect PhD programs fear being seen merely as "professional" schools, in the way law, medical, and business schools are. But aside from the obvious snobbery of this position, department heads would do well to remember that academia is just as much a profession as any other, with the rather mundane elements of paychecks, promotions, benefits, and retirement plans, and that there is just as much an obligation to teach its students about *getting work in* and *working within* the profession as there is to make them "well-rounded," "knowledgeable" instructors in the humanities. (Graff 1994: 12)

Adding to this dilemma, then--that writing is often the most demanding but essential task in an academic career--is the fact that instruction in academic writing is difficult to come by. Some graduate students, especially those in the sciences and other fields where co-authorship is the norm, are fortunate enough to receive guidance from a mentor. In fields such as the humanities, however, where co-authorship is not as widely practiced, the graduate student or beginning assistant professor is typically left on his or her own to figure out the intricacies of academic publication--often with dire results, when understanding comes too late or not at all.

This is not to say that the faculty in these fields do not require writing of their graduate students. In fact, faculty (especially in the humanities) regularly require students to write papers. The problem is that they rarely show them how to do it--and even more rarely, how to prepare it for a public forum such as a conference presentation or a journal publication. Instead, too often the scenario in a graduate seminar runs something like the following:

Chapter 1: Introduction

(1) during the first week of classes the professor assigns a paper which will be due the last week of classes;

(2) little mention is made of the assignment, other than potential topics, during the remaining weeks;

(3) the student begins and writes the paper within one or two weeks of its due date;

(4) the professor gives most of the papers A's and B's, even while shuddering at their generally poor quality;

(5) the student files the paper away and never looks at it again.

Another problem is that, when it comes to composing, there's a seemingly infinite amount of information for a potential writer to learn. Note that most composition handbooks and texts for technical and business writing attempt to cover everything there is to know: many approach a thousand pages in length. However, we feel it's unrealistic and unproductive to try to master every detail and nuance of writing for publication at once.

As an alternative, over the past seven years we have developed courses at our respective universities, variously titled "Writing about Writing," "Language and Writing," and so forth. The common core of these courses has been twofold: (1) to expose students to the various methods of analyzing academic discourse; and (2) to show them how to begin doing--and

Chapter 1: Introduction

publishing--such work themselves. We concentrate on a handful of assignments which can be taught (but not necessarily mastered) in one semester and practiced throughout a student's graduate and professional career. To this end, we typically require each student to produce five pieces of work in a one-semester course:

(1) a book review, such as one would submit to an academic journal

(2) an abstract, such as one would submit as the basis for a conference presentation

(3) an oral presentation, such as one would make at a professional conference

(4) a critical article, such as one would write in response to a single published paper

(5) a research article, articulating original work.

We focus on these items because they are, by and large, the most common types of published academic writing. That is, around a university, these are the basic types of writing that one must master in order to survive.

It is remarkable that once they are given some practical, hands-on instruction, many students can produce good quality, publishable work in the space of a few semesters. Consider just a few examples of students who were able to take the critical step of beginning to publish while still in school:

A.D.M. (Ph.D. Linguistics, 1988). As a graduate student, published articles in *Lingua*, *Language Sciences*, *Semiotica*, and *Journal of Technical Writing and Communication*. Has had three tenure-track job offers. Now an associate professor at Brigham Young University.

K.S.F. (B.S. Computer Science, 1989). As an undergraduate, published an article in *Journal of Technical Writing and Communication* and a review in *TESOL Quarterly*. Now on full scholarship at Harvard, with a Ph.D. in linguistics expected 1995.

K.S.C. (Ph.D. English, 1990). As a graduate student, published articles in *Journal of Business Communication*, *Educational Research Quarterly*, *Language Quarterly*, and *Journal of Technical Writing and Communication*, and a review in *College Composition and Communication*. Has had two tenure-track job offers. Now an associate professor at the Air Force Institute of Technology.

D.G.W. (Ph.D. English, 1994). As a graduate student, published articles in *Language and Style*, *Science Fiction Studies*, and *Auto/biography Studies*. Now a fellow at the North Carolina Center for the Advancement of Teaching.

It's not uncommon for such students to command nine-month salaries in the $50,000 range just a few years out of graduate school, even in the traditionally low-paying humanities. And the simple fact is that they owe their success to their ability to write and publish in respectable journals, virtually at will.

Chapter 1: Introduction

This book consolidates our best advice about learning how to produce some of the basic forms of academic discourse: the book review, the abstract, the conference presentation, the response article, and the research article. Each chapter covers one of these forms, with several chapters devoted to various elements of the research article. Within each chapter, we have attempted to articulate principles and to examine in detail both successful and unsuccessful examples of the genre under discussion.

We do not pretend to include everything that could be said about these genres, nor do we pretend that everything we say applies equally to every academic field. In fact, most of our examples come from reviews, conference papers, and articles pertaining to discourse analysis, an area within the field of linguistics. We do believe, however, that the principles advanced in this book can be generalized to provide most beginning academics with the essentials of writing for publication in their respective fields.

Chapter 2: The Book Review

We begin with book reviews because they are the easiest and quickest form of publishable academic writing. They are relatively easy because the reviewer has only to read a book, not generate an original idea. Reviews are relatively quick to write because they are short: they vary in length from roughly 500 to 1500 words. (So-called "review essays" can be much longer, and consequently look more like full-blown articles than reviews.)

There are several ways to get started in writing book reviews. Most journals do not accept unsolicited reviews (i.e., reviews that are sent in by the writer without first having been solicited by the editor). This means you'll have to get the editor's approval first. Once you've decided on a book you'd like to review, write the editor to ask if he or she would be interested in publishing a review of that book. The editor will then write back accepting or declining your offer.

Some journals (e.g., *Language*) actually publish a list of "Books Received," which are books that they have received from publishers and that are available for review. Even if a journal does not publish such a list, you can let the editor know that you are available to write reviews on a particular subject area. The editor may then send you a book to review when he or she receives one in that area. (An added bonus is that the reviewer traditionally receives the book under review for free.)

Chapter 2: The Book Review

Three types of academic books are available for review: scholarly books, textbooks, and collections of articles. We advise against beginning graduate students trying to review scholarly books. Such works require too much background knowledge on the part of the reviewer. Textbooks, on the other hand, are relatively easy to review. You can, for example, review a book for one of your courses. Better yet, if you used a particular textbook in one of your courses, read *another* textbook that could have been used for the same course and review it. The new book will be easier to evaluate because you'll have something to compare it to. Likewise, collections are a good place to start. They are relatively easy to describe--a list of the articles and the main point of each--and journal editors seem to have more trouble finding reviewers for collections, which means there's less competition for you--the potential reviewer.

Once you agree to write a review, allow yourself at least a month to do the whole job: two weeks to read the book, a week to digest it, and a week to write the review. This may sound like too much time to allot for a simple review, but you have to allow for some lost time. (We take up time management in more detail in the next chapter.)

In the following sections we will discuss sample reviews of textbooks and collections.

Textbooks

Minimally, a textbook review should contain at least the following components: a DESCRIPTION (including chapter titles),

Chapter 2: The Book Review

the PURPOSE of the book (what courses is it for?), two or three notable STRENGTHS and WEAKNESSES, and an overall EVALUATION (is it useful or not?). Consider, for example, the following review of Kaplan's *English Grammar*, written by Riley for the journal *Language*. (Descriptive headings have been added in the margin.)

English Grammar: Principles and Facts. By JEFFREY P. KAPLAN. Englewood Cliffs, NJ: Prentice-Hall, 1989. Pp. x, 358. Cloth $31.67.

DESCRIPTION

  Kaplan's textbook is designed for `classes in English grammar or in linguistics focussing on English' (x). It offers chapters on `Some ways of thinking about grammar', `The structure of English sound', `The structure of English words', `Parts of speech', `Nouns and verbs: Subclasses and features', `Phrase structure', `Grammatical relations', `Complex sentences', `Relative clauses and participles', and `Anaphora'.

PURPOSE

  Given its emphasis on syntax, this book would not be the best choice for an introductory survey of linguistics; it would need to include more discussion of semantics, pragmatics, and applied areas. However, for courses in grammar, syntax, or the structure of English, K's text has several

STRENGTHS

strengths. Most importantly, K accurately discusses a wide range of syntactic phenomena. He also introduces the student to argumentation, rather than simply listing `facts.' Numerous exercises appear within and at the end of each chapter. And K does a good job of integrating traditional grammar, standard theory, and more recent innovations (e.g., X' theory). This eclecticism makes more sense than excluding useful descriptive devices simply because they are not state of the art.

Chapter 2: The Book Review

WEAKNESSES

At the same time, *English Grammar* does display some flaws in organization and coverage. Although Chapter 1 begins clearly enough by contrasting prescriptive and descriptive approaches, it loses unity by treating other topics prematurely (e.g., language variation and language change) and in too much detail (e.g., a technical discussion of consonant cluster reduction). More generally, the book's adherence to the usual `bottom-up' organization (phonology-morphology-syntax) conflicts with its focus on syntax. K describes Chapters 4-7 as the book's core; if so, then why not move Chapters 2 and 3, on phonology and morphology, to an appendix, and start the student off with more accessible material on syntax? (`Grammatical Relations' would make an excellent earlier chapter, since it elaborates on familiar concepts such as subject and object.) The chapters on syntax likewise display some unevenness. For example, much of Chapter 4, `Parts of Speech,' reappears in later chapters. Chapter 6, `Phrase Structure,' allots 9 pages to analyzing the phrase structure of *a white horse*, but only 11 pages to 8 `non-canonical' sentence types: negatives, *yes-no*, *wh-*, and tag questions, imperatives, preposed constructions, inversions, and existential *there*. This latter material deserves more treatment.

Another oddity is K's ambivalence about transformations. He claims to use them `only implicitly,' in order `to avoid bogging down in the theory-driven details of derivations and transformational formalizations' (x). In fact, however, K relies throughout on concepts such as `underlying structure' (as in pre-dative movement), `derivations' (as of imperatives), `processes' (such as raising), `movement' (as through passivization), and `rules' (such as five steps for deriving tag questions). And K certainly introduces details and formalism when discussing phonology, morphology, phrase structure rules (e.g., 216-217),

Chapter 2: The Book Review

EVALUATION

and tree structures (e.g., 285, 291). It is not clear, then, what he gains by avoiding a direct discussion of the concept `transformation.'

In sum, *English Grammar* covers a wide range of syntactic phenomena appropriate for an introductory course in the structure of English. However, instructors may want to modify the book's emphasis and organization at some points. (Riley 1991: 867-68)

This review follows the fairly conventional organization described above: DESCRIPTION, PURPOSE, STRENGTHS, WEAKNESSES, EVALUATION. Note, in addition, that this review implies more of a negative assessment of the text than it actually states. First, note that Riley devotes twice as much space to the book's weaknesses as she does to its strengths. Second, note that the best she has to say about the book in her final evaluation is that it's "appropriate" for a particular course.

Now consider a review of the same text, written by Alan Manning for the American Dialect Society's *Teaching Newsletter*. You will see that his review contains the same essential elements as Riley's, although it follows a different organization.

Jeffrey P. Kaplan, *English Grammar: Principles and Facts*, Englewood Cliffs, NJ: Prentice Hall, 1989, 358 pp., including index.

Assessment: The first three of its ten chapters deal with language variation, phonology, and morphology, and it "presupposes no previous experience with linguistics" (x), but *English Grammar* is best suited to a second undergraduate or perhaps a beginning graduate

Chapter 2: The Book Review

course focused on English syntax. For the most part, *EG* introduces linguistic terms, discusses the concepts and reinforces them with exercises, but the variety of concepts covered is ambitious (e.g., a discussion of logical truth tables is worked into the chapter on parts of speech). Also, the prose, though lucid and at times entertaining, often becomes laden with parenthetical ideas:

> Traditionally, **gerunds** are verbal nouns, meaning that they are nouns derived from verbs. They have the same form as present participles, being composed of a verb stem and a suffixed -ing (*running, swimming, studying*, etc., are all both participles and gerunds). "Gerund" comes, interestingly enough, from the word *gerundum*, itself a gerund of the Latin verb *gerere*, "to carry on" (that is, the ancestor of the grammatical term was an example of itself). (p. 135)

I find this style tempting myself, but it can be daunting for students still unaccustomed to the terms and careful reading. Hence, I would use *EG* to review and expand upon ideas students have already been exposed to.

Methods: Chapters 4-7, on parts of speech, nouns and verbs, phrase structure, and case relationships, make up the "core" of *EG*. K discusses phrasal and transformational principles without relying on formal rules. He uses short exercises to drill many (but not all) concepts previously discussed. In Chapter 6, for example, several types of transformation are presented as "non-canonical" sentence forms—negatives, questions, Wh-questions, tag-questions, fronted phrases, inversion, and existential *there* sentences—followed by these exercise prompts:

> Propose "logical" forms for the following wh-questions, putting the wh-words in their "logical" positions. (Example: the logical form for *who(m) did Max visit* is *Max visited who(m)*).... (p. 236)

> Some occurrences of *be* are auxes, and some are main verbs. Which kind of *be* does the logical subject of an existential *there* sentence go after, or does it matter? Here are some data sentences.... (p. 241)

Chapter 2: The Book Review

> **Strong Features:** Each chapter is well-organized and logically subdivided with headings, subheadings, and exercises. *EG* represents a commendable effort to bring some more advanced syntactic principles to an introductory text: for example, the concepts of N-bar and V-bar, c-command, anaphora, and some useful introductory discussion of suprasegmentals and hierarchical structure in morphology.
>
> **Weak Features:** *EG* would have been improved with a glossary. Besides the dense style, exercises are somewhat uneven in coverage and sophistication; many effectively review concepts, but some are a little too advanced or open-ended, for example:
>
>> Write a short paper explaining to a friend who has not had linguistics one of the following ideas... (p. 241)
>>
>> For each underlined word or phrase in the following passages, say everything you can about it... (p. 189).
>
> (Manning 1993: 3-4)

Manning's review follows a less conventional format. For example, his DESCRIPTION of the book is spaced over two sections: what he labels *Assessment* ("The first three of its ten chapters deal with language variation, phonology, and morphology . . . .") and *Methods* ("Chapters 4-7, on parts of speech, nouns and verbs, phrase structure, and case relationships, make up the `core' of *English Grammar*"). Nonetheless, this review has three properties that promote its effectiveness. First, it begins (rather than ends) with an EVALUATION (*Assessment*). This way Manning provides a frame of reference, making it easier for the reader to process details that come later. In essence, the reader knows where Manning stands right from the outset. Second, Manning uses headings (i.e., *Assessment, Methods, Strong Features, Weak Features*) to make the structure of the review more transparent to the reader.

Finally, it contains one or two well-chosen examples form the textbook itself to illustrate the main point in each section. For instance, Manning exemplifies Kaplan's dense writing style with a quote from the text about the word *gerund* and its etymology.

Keep in mind that the fundamental question a reader brings to a textbook review is "Can I use this book in my course on such-and-such?" The reviewer's job is to answer this question. Particular items that are of interest to readers of textbook reviews include the clarity of the textbook's definitions, the balance between generalizations and examples, the clarity of the organization and format (e.g., use of headings and other methods of highlighting important points), and the number and nature of exercises, problems, or questions for students. Thus, your review of a textbook should try to address as many of these points as possible.

Collections

A few years ago Sarah Thomason, the editor of *Language*, gave readers advice on how to review edited collections of papers. Here are some excerpts from her column:

(1) "a review of an edited collection, like any other review, should be evaluative as well as descriptive."

(2) "give up the idea of listing and describing every paper. . . . characterize the book as a whole."

(3) "[W]hat were the editor's goals, and how well were they achieved?" [Consult the editor's overview in the opening chapter.]

Chapter 2: The Book Review

    (4)   "What are the major themes of the book?" [Are there recurrent topics or overriding ideas?]

    (5)   "If the book is a conference [proceedings], how well do the papers represent the conference topic?" (1990: 659)

With these guidelines in mind, consider the following excerpts from a review by Alice Ann Fesmire, written when she was a graduate student. The volume under review is a collection of essays on the question of establishing English as the official language of the U.S.

Not Only English: Affirming America's Multilingual Heritage, edited by Harvey A. Daniels, Urbana, IL: National Council of Teachers of English, 1990. 135 pp.

    The English-only movement in the United States is a political question having much to do with immigration policy, education policy, racism, and civil liberties, and little to do with linguistic practices of Americans. Accordingly, this book is a political statement by the National Council of Teachers of English (NCTE), through its Commission on Language, which attempts to explain the NCTE's position on the issue and "provide the kinds of historical, linguistic, and educational background necessary to understand and *combat* language restrictionism" [p. viii, emphasis added.]

    The editor, Harvey A. Daniels, education professor and chair of interdisciplinary studies at National-Louis University, writes two of the twelve essays which comprise the book's chapters. Ten other educators and scholars were invited to contribute the remaining chapters. The essays are grouped into four sections: 1) The Nature and Origins of the English-Only Movement, 2) The Dangers of Official-English Laws, 3) The Deeper Meanings of Language Restrictionism, and 4) Responding to the English-Only Movement.

    The first section provides an overview of the problem and discusses the historical background of the debate. Daniels' first essay

Chapter 2: The Book Review

is on language protectionism, and it concludes that "the English-only movement was built on misinformation, ignorance, and fear, but not on hatred" [p. 11]. Daniels blames the movement on misguided but well-meaning, patriotic Americans. . . .

In her chapter, Elizabeth Frick examines the motives behind the metaphors using water images that consistently imply a "*disaster by water*: a flood, a tide, a flow, a wave, a stream, a deluge, an inundation that threatens to drown the country" [p. 27]. Frick evidently interprets the Sapir-Whorf theory to mean that language causes reality, but although the water images are interesting, they are not marked for negative connotation out of context. For example, a "wave of immigrants" or a "stream of people" from a particular country is a frightening image to a xenophobe, but could be downright refreshing to a resident of a desert, to follow that line of thinking. Frick overstates her conclusion that anti-immigrant rhetoric creates a climate of hatred which helped cause a sniper to open fire in a schoolyard, killing Southeast Asian immigrant children because he hated Asian immigrants. Rational thinkers can distinguish between inflammatory rhetoric and murder. . . .

[Summaries of eight other essays follow.]

In sum, this book is a political treatise by a professional organization whose purpose is to defeat the ELA in any federal or state form. Educators and others who wish to inform themselves on the English-only movement will find one side of the issue presented in this book. The rhetoric is consistently militant and strident (*combat, disaster, aftermath, marshalling, fight*, etc.). Despite contributions by some applied linguists, there is no analysis from the theoretical linguist's point of view. Again, and significantly, this is not an issue about language at all. Nevertheless, a theoretical linguist could add to the argument by emphasizing the organic nature of language and the inevitability of its growth and evolution. Another shortcoming of the book is the lack of a glossary identifying organizations and key figures. There is initial confusion about U.S. English, Tanton, EPIC, and other crucial pieces of the puzzle for the reader who begins with only a vague familiarity with the English-only movement and S. I. Hayakawa. The lack of such background is an indication that this book is not intended for a general audience, but is instead a political

Chapter 2: The Book Review

> manifesto explicating the party line for members of the profession. (Fesmire 1992: 223-26)

The structure of this review is simple and straightforward: the first two paragraphs serve as a general DESCRIPTION of the book; the last paragraph serves as an EVALUATION; and the intervening paragraphs describe and evaluate each essay, one by one.

There are two things to note about this review. First, if Fesmire had wanted or needed to shorten her review, she could have done so by including only one *representative* paper from each of the four sections. That is, she could have described and evaluated four papers rather than twelve. Second, Fesmire not only describes each individual essay, she evaluates it as well. Note, for example, that in her treatment of Frick's paper in the fourth paragraph, she says "Frick overstates her conclusion." Likewise, "Frick evidently interprets . . ." suggests that Frick's interpretation is wrong. Finally, Fesmire closes with "Rational thinkers can distinguish between . . ." implying that Frick cannot.

Now consider Parker's review of the proceedings of an American-Soviet conference on language. In this case, however, the reviewer does not try to describe all thirteen papers in the collection. Instead, he generalizes from the papers themselves and reviews only five of the papers as *representative examples* of his generalization.

Chapter 2: The Book Review

Language Typology 1985: Papers from the Linguistic Typology Symposium, Moscow, 9-13 December 1985. Ed. Winfred P. Lehmann. Amsterdam: John Benjamins Publishing Company, 1986. viii + 209 pp. $32.00.

DESCRIPTION

This collection consists of the revised forms of 13 papers prepared by Soviet and American scholars for the Colloquium in Linguistic Typology held in Moscow on December 9-13, 1985. It was planned that the colloquium would cover eight topics of interest to typologists. The topics and the authors who treat them are: (1) Primes (Lehmann, Yartseva); (2) What is language type? (Solntsev, Klimov); (3) Form versus content (Nichols, Kibrik); (4) Metalanguages (Timberlake); (5) Commensurability of terms (Harris); (6) Different structures and their relevance to typology (Gamkrelidze); (7) Areal typology (Austerlitz, Krauss); and (8) Typological shift (Gukhman, Hopper). The conference, as the first meeting of the two delegations, was "designed to acquaint scholars of each country with one another's contributions" (viii).

PURPOSE

GENERALIZATION

This collection does, in fact, reveal quite a bit about differences between American and Soviet scholarship--not so much in terms of content but in terms of academic style. As a group, the American papers tend to be narrow, concrete, and focussed on specific details, while the Soviet essays tend to be broad, abstract, and concerned with a general overview. These differences are reflected in length: the seven papers by Americans average 20 pages, while the six papers by Soviets average only seven pages. In fact, Soviet authorship constitutes less than 25% of the text.

STRENGTHS

The papers themselves run the gamut between the best and worst of both approaches to scholarship. Alice Harris's "Commensurability of

Terms" strikes a desirable balance between a general thesis and specific evidence. She states her thesis clearly: "Since most typological studies depend upon primary analysis of individual languages, the typologist must take into consideration differences in the use of terms in these descriptions and the effects these differences may have on the analysis" (55). Her comparison of English and Russian terminology includes a treatment of *typology, agglutinative, inflectional, synthetic, analytic, prefixing, suffixing, class, gender, ergativity, voice,* and *complementation*. Her discussion of the terminology used to distinguish nominative-accusative construction from ergative-absolutive is especially useful. Likewise, Johanna Nichols's paper, "On Form and Content in Typology," represents the best of both schools of scholarship. . . .

WEAKNESSES

Unfortunately, however, not all of the papers balance a general thesis and specific evidence. Many of the Americans' papers reflect a preoccupation with detail at the expense of relevant generalization. Timberlake's paper on "Metalanguage," for example, deals with its stated topic only tangentially; instead, he offers a system for handling thematic relations based on Fillmore's case grammar. And this we do not discover until 15 pages into his 28-page article. Austerlitz's "Areal Phonetic Typology in Time: North and East Asia" and Krauss's "A Survey of Major Alaskan Language Types" are full of well-organized information, but these topics seem too narrow for a collection of this type. . . .

At the opposite end of the spectrum, many of the Soviet contributors present a clearly articulated outline but fail to provide supporting detail. Gamkrelidze's "Lexico-semantic Reconstruction and the Linguistic Paleontology of Culture" is an interesting attempt to practice social history through

Chapter 2: The Book Review

linguistics. The author describes the object of such research as "not the proto-language but the proto-culture . . . . what is reconstructed is not so much the language itself as the extra-linguistic world reflected in the linguistic data" (44). Without specific examples, however, it is difficult to see how such research might be done. Kibrik's "The Meaning-Form Correspondence in Grammatical Description" also generalizes at the expense of supporting detail. . . .

EVALUATION

In sum, this volume is of interest primarily because of what it reveals about the different styles of scholarship practiced by Americans and Soviets. Among the former, the big picture tends to get lost amid a wealth of detail; among the latter, supporting evidence is suppressed until only a bare outline of an argument remains. Thus, this collection will interest only a small number of typologists working on one of the topics treated in the book, and perhaps philosophers of science. Word order typologists and general linguists will probably not find enough of interest in the volume to justify its relatively high price. Likewise, I cannot envision assigning the entire book to graduate students in a typology seminar.

One final note: in his preface, Lehmann solicits suggestions for planning the second meeting of these two delegations. I have this to offer. First, choose a half dozen or so topics that will interest typologists in general (e.g., "typological shift" but not "different structures and their relevance to typology"; either "commensurability of terms" or "metalanguage," but not both). Second, ask one American and one Soviet participant to respond to each topic with a survey of the research literature. Third, ask each author to draw one single generalization from this survey and support it with concrete detail. The resulting volume will be of interest not only to a small group of

Chapter 2: The Book Review

> specialists but to typologists of all persuasions and their students. (Parker 1988: 117-19)

Note that after a DESCRIPTION of the collection and a statement of its PURPOSE (in the editor's own words), the reviewer creates a GENERALIZATION: American scholarship is narrow, concrete, and specific, while Soviet scholarship is broad, abstract, and general. This allows the reviewer to pick out the best and worst of both approaches. On the one hand, Harris's and Nichols's papers balance specific facts with general conclusions (STRENGTHS). On the other hand, Timberlake's, Austerlitz's, and Krauss's are too specific, while Gamkrelidze's and Kibrik's are too general (WEAKNESSES). The last two paragraphs of the review constitute the EVALUATION, which includes advice for the organizers of future such meetings between the Americans and the Soviets.

To summarize, a review of a collection can take primarily a descriptive or an evaluative approach. Fesmire's review illustrates the former, since her discussion is organized primarily by the order of the essays in the book. Parker's review illustrates that latter, since his discussion is organized primarily by the "strengths--weaknesses" dichotomy.

Before leaving the subject of reviews, we would urge those beginning their professional careers to avoid any sort of inflammatory rhetoric. The following comments, for example, come from a review of a collection of papers on Southern speech:

> "This anthology is as stimulating as a yawning contest and has the freshness of a smoked Virginia ham."

Chapter 2: The Book Review

"the collection [has] all of the focus of a scattershot blast from a shotgun."

"If this book were a potential Broadway play, it would have gone into rewrites after a one-night flop in Baltimore." (Underwood, 1988: 143-44)

There is nothing wrong with using rhetoric like this if you are secure enough in your own career to risk alienating the author(s) you are reviewing (and possibly some readers). Personally, we believe that the review from which these excerpts are taken is accurate and, incidentally, one of the most entertaining we have read. However, it was written by a seasoned tenured professor who was apparently willing to make enemies. Obviously, graduate students or those early in their careers would be risking a lot to "burn bridges" in this fashion.

Chapter 3: Time Management

The most important ingredient in completing and publishing research is time. It takes approximately three months working part-time to research and write a 20-page manuscript which is worthy of submission to a professional journal. It's important to emphasize that this type of work has to be performed part-time. It's virtually impossible for anyone to spend more than two to four hours a day reading articles or writing. (Almost everyone has tried at one time or another to write a term paper in a week or less; this is why it never works.)

Unfortunately, though, time is a limited commodity for most beginning professionals. And, admittedly, most of us don't make the most effective use of the time we've got. In this chapter, we want to suggest some ways to make the most productive use of that time. In order to do so, we'll take a general look at four stages that typically comprise the process of composing an article, from getting the initial idea to producing the manuscript for submission to a journal. Each of these stages, in turn, culminates in one product: an abstract, a conference paper, a first draft of an article, and a final draft.

In subsequent chapters we will look in more detail at examples of these products. For now, we'll limit our discussion to an overview of each one. We will focus on the relative amount of time, over a period of three months, that you should realistically expect to devote to each step in producing a

Chapter 3: Time Management

research article, and on some strategies for using that time effectively.

Stage I: Random Reading (one month)

The primary purpose of this stage is to generate an idea for a paper. Your goal at the end of this stage is to have a commitment to a topic. The only way to do this is simply to read around in the field. You need to spend an hour or so every other day in the library looking through recent issues of professional journals that are likely to contain articles relevant to your field. Our interest is in analyzing written discourse, so we would concentrate on journals such as *Journal of Technical Writing and Communication*, *Technical Communication Quarterly*, *Journal of Business Communication*, *Journal of Business and Technical Communication*, *Technical Communication*, *English for Specific Purposes*, *IEEE Transactions on Professional Communication*, *Written Communication*, and *College Composition and Communication*. You should be able to make a similar list of the top five or ten journals in your field. If not, consult with a professor or colleague for journal titles.

In any recent issue of a journal, read the table of contents. If a title looks interesting, read the abstract. If the abstract looks interesting, skim the article. If the article seems useful, copy it, including all the relevant bibliographical information (year, volume, journal), and keep it on file wherever you do your work--home or office. It's a good idea to keep on an index card the bibliographical information for every article, book, or book chapter you read. It's a virtual certainty that later on in the writing process you will want to cite some item from your early reading, and these cards will prove invaluable then.

You should try to read an average of one article a day, including weekends. We have found that, in the long run, this type of work is easier to complete if you do a little every day. (The same principle applies to the writing stages that we will discuss later.) That is, instead of trying to read seven articles in one day, aim for reading one article every day. Because research is a complex and difficult task, our natural inclination is to put it off as long as possible. The problem is, it's possible to put it off indefinitely! The best way we've found to avoid this problem is to put in an hour or two of work each morning, *first thing*.

As you go through the reading process, you will slowly start to identify the pressing questions in the field and the major references. For example, if you're researching the field of written discourse, you will start to notice Halliday and Hasan's *Cohesion in English* over and over again in the references section of the articles you read. You will also notice repeated references to issues such as process vs. product, cohesion vs. coherence, and research vs. pedagogy. Also, be on the lookout for references in the literature to unsolved problems or unanswered questions. Such questions are often raised toward the conclusion of an article. For example, in her paper "Speech Act Theory and Degrees of Directness in Professional Writing," Riley speculates on the relative contribution of various indirectness markers to the perception of politeness:

Chapter 3: Time Management

> [This] raises the question of whether they are equally indirect: i.e., is adding a hedge to a question equivalent to adding a pessimism marker to a question? This remains, for the time, an unresolved issue, and perhaps a relevant subject for researchers in professional communication to investigate. Research in speech act theory has not, to my knowledge, constructed a clear picture of how (or if) these various individual strategies should be ranked on some scale of intrinsic politeness." (1988a: 16).

This, of course, is a ready-made topic for an article, and in fact, one of Parker's students, Zaixin Zhang, investigated this exact question and published the results in an article entitled "Ranking of Indirectness in Professional Writing" two years after Riley's article appeared.

The point is that if you work diligently, at the end of a month, you will have at least a topic (e.g., politeness in professional correspondence) or at best a thesis (e.g., politeness is a function of indirectness). At the end of this stage you will be able to write a 200-word abstract and submit it to the organizers of a professional conference, so they can consider it for presentation at a later date. (More on abstracts and conference presentations in chapters 4 and 5.) The main things to keep in mind during this stage are (1) read an article a day (i.e., 30 in a month) and (2) keep a record of everything you read.

Stage II: Focussed Reading (one month)

The primary function of this stage is to collect and organize the information you will need to write up your idea. Your goals at the end of this stage are to be committed to a thesis and to have gathered evidence in support of it. During this stage all of your reading should be restricted solely to your idea. For example, if you're going to write about tone, then reading about another topic, such as cohesion, is probably irrelevant. At this stage, you can't afford to get sidetracked by reading on subjects that are not directly related to your idea, no matter how interesting.

Your first task is to collect relevant articles. Begin by going through the articles you read during your month of random reading and pick out those that deal with your idea. Go through the references at the end of each of these articles and try to identify any relevant reading you have missed. If you can find a recent article (i.e., one published within the last two years) on your topic, it should contain most of the major references you'll need. You should also make a systematic search at the time through the bibliographies and indexes in your field. This will alert you to titles that you might have missed, especially in journals that your library may not have, and will give you time to order these through inter-library loan.

At this stage you should be open to articles that present a variety of viewpoints and types of evidence about your topic. Pay special attention to researchers whose perspective you disagree with; you will need to address their perspective in your article and, as we will see in the chapter on Introductions, you can often use an opposing viewpoint as an springboard into your own thesis. Also pay special attention to any evidence you encounter that your topic hasn't been treated as fully as it could. In fact, one thing you should be monitoring during the focussed reading stage is the *absence* of research about your topic.

Chapter 3: Time Management

Eventually you can use this to argue for the significance of your own treatment.

Second, go through the articles you've assembled that deal with your idea. Read each article (again, if necessary) making notes in the margin and highlighting passages that you may want to quote or evidence that you may want to cite in your paper.

Third, go back through these articles and copy any material (i.e., facts, quotes) that you think you might use in your paper onto note cards. As you copy the material, make a brief note of its significance (i.e., what the material might be used as evidence for). Each card should contain (1) one and only one fact/quote, (2) the author, year, and page number from which it is taken, (3) the relevance of the fact/quote, and (4) the main point in red at the top.

Figure 3.1 shows an example of one of the cards we used in collecting material for a book on politeness and clarity in professional writing. This card contains a quote from page 109 of a 1984 article by Houlette. (The complete bibliographical entry for this article is on another card, so we know exactly which article the quote is from.) At the top of the card is the point we will make with this quote, namely that composition researchers equate linguistics with empiricism. At the bottom of the card is our interpretation of this quote, namely that Houlette equates linguistics with empiricism and defines empiricism as having to do with behaviorism, measurement, and enumeration. Note that we have underlined the relevant words in the quote, so that we can pick them out easily when we get ready to use the information on this card.

Chapter 3: Time Management

Linguistics = Empiricism

"<u>Empiricism</u>, when applied to composition research, must inherently take a <u>linguistic</u> or <u>behavioral</u> approach to discourse because of the emphasis on <u>measurement</u>. In order to measure some feature of a text or its impact on a reader, we must be able to convert aspects of the text or of the response to <u>numbers</u>." (Houlette, 1984, 109; emphasis added)

Passage establishes connection that many compositionists implicitly assume to exist between linguistics and empiricism. Author equates "linguistic" approach with "behavioral approach," which is further equated with measurement, enumeration, and ultimately empiricism.

Figure 3.1. Sample Note Card

It may seem unnecessary to transfer your marginal notes and quotations to these cards. However, this step is crucial to ensure that later you will be able to *rearrange* the information on the cards in the order in which it will appear in your paper. It's impossible to accomplish this task if you have numerous notes on a single sheet of paper. Remember, too, to compile a separate note card containing complete bibliographic information for each new source you encounter.

If you perform the work at this stage diligently, at the end of the second month you will be able to prepare a conference presentation based on your idea. The main thing to keep in mind at this stage is to get each piece of information you might use in your paper onto a note card, complete with enough bibliographical information so that you won't have to return to the original source.

Chapter 3: Time Management

Stage III: First Draft (two weeks)

The primary purpose of this stage is to translate your research into the format of an article. This is often the most difficult step in writing an article. Researching an idea and later revising the written product are not major stumbling blocks for most writers; it's actually getting that first draft on paper that is most difficult. However, this stage can be relatively simple if Stages I and II were done thoroughly. In fact, much of your task will consist of organizing and copying the material from the cards onto paper (or disk). Remember that each card contains, among other things, a *fact or quote* and *your interpretation of its significance*. Thus, you will end up with each point you want to make, followed by evidence or an illustration--not just a string of unrelated quotes or a series of unsupported, unillustrated points.

The process of transferring your cards onto paper or disk should be done without regard for precise wording. Once this is done, you can reorganize as necessary and add transitions, then add an introduction and conclusion. Once the whole draft is blocked out on paper, the very last thing to do is to revise at the sentence and word levels.

The main thing to keep in mind at this stage is to make your argument transparent. You've got to be hard on yourself; if the logic of your article isn't crystal clear to you, it won't be clear to anyone else. Remember that there is an endless number of things to read; if the organization of yours is the least bit hard to follow, your reader will put it down and pick up something else.

Stage IV: Final Draft (two weeks)

The primary purpose of this stage is to solicit criticism and revise accordingly. Before submitting your manuscript to a journal, try to get someone competent to read it and give you some feedback. We say "try" because it is often difficult to find someone who is willing and able to critique another person's writing. We know of a case where, after submitting a paper for a graduate course, the student was called by the instructor, who said "Excellent work, but where is the footnote page?" The student replied "Dr. _____, the footnotes are at the bottom of each page of text." It was obvious that the instructor had not bothered to read the paper before awarding it an A.

Several strategies may help to increase your odds of getting a useful response when asking a colleague or professor to critique a manuscript. First, give the person at least a week to look over the manuscript. Set up an appointment for a specific day and time at which you will return to discuss the article. Second, ask for feedback on particular areas (e.g., your use of examples) or sections of the manuscript. This will give the reader some specific points to focus on. Third, give the reader some idea of what you want to do with the manuscript-- for example, what journal you plan to submit it to, or at least what audience you are trying to reach.

If you are lucky enough to get feedback, you need to accept it graciously and assess it judiciously. Sometimes a reader's comment will make no sense to you at all. If so, you can ask for clarification; if it still makes no sense, you have no choice but to ignore it. On the other hand, if two readers make the same criticism, it is probably accurate and you'll need to address it. Under no circumstances, however, should you argue with a reader, interrupting him or her with what you "really wanted to say."

This drive to be defensive in the face of criticism runs deep. In a recent column in *College Composition and Communication*, the journal's editor, Richard Gebhardt, noted the disturbing "tendency of authors to argue, in later drafts, with comments referees made about earlier drafts of their submissions. A few authors, in fact, have used their readers' revision recommendations, not to revise their work but to launch new papers incorporating--and usually challenging--the referees' comments" (1993: 439). Likewise, in a recent "Forum" column in *PMLA*, the official journal of the Modern Language Association, Edward LeComte noted a similar trend among authors: "they react with not always muted rage . . . when corrections or suggestions for expansion are offered; any questions raised are treated as personal insults, despicable and malicious assaults . . . . An impersonal interest in getting things right is outside their conception" (1994: 443). The message here is clear: if the reader doesn't get your point, fix the prose, not the reader.

Another important strategy as you are preparing your final draft is to put the manuscript aside for several days and then come back and read it "fresh." It's easy to become enamored of your own prose or entangled in faulty logic while you're in the midst of preparing a draft. Working on other projects for a few days will allow you to get some distance on the manuscript and view it from a more dispassionate perspective.

Chapter 3: Time Management

At this stage, the most difficult changes to make are those involving reorganization. Nonetheless, it's better to "bite the bullet" and deal with the problem immediately rather than send the paper out and get it rejected with the comment that "the last paragraph on page 10 should come before the middle paragraph on page 8." For example, Parker wrote a paper in graduate school and submitted it for publication. After it was rejected twice, he realized that the paper really consisted of two papers in one. The two papers were disjoined (parts 1 and 3 were one paper and part 2 was another) and sent to different journals, *Journal of Speech and Hearing Disorders* and *Lingua*, where each was accepted for publication without further change.

Oftentimes the easiest way to solve an organization problem is to delete something--sometimes a sentence or paragraph, sometimes a whole section. Deleting part of what you've written is exceedingly difficult psychologically. Writers always hate to get rid of something that they've gone to the trouble to write. One of our colleagues, Tom Walsh, suggests doing it in stages. First, if you're working on a computer, block off the material you're thinking about deleting and move it to the end of the document. A week or so later, it will be easier to delete when you see it out of context.

On the other hand, you may have to supplement a particular section with additional quotations or facts. At this point you can go through your note cards for that section. Any unused card may provide you with supplemental information. (Note how difficult this would be if you had to sift through your original sources looking randomly for relevant quotes--this is why we told you to transfer your material to note cards in Stage II.)

Chapter 3: Time Management

The following anecdote illustrates the value of transferring such information to note cards. Recently, Parker was directing an M.A. thesis for a student who moved to another state before her thesis was finished. During the semester she was trying to graduate, two of her committee members asked her to add supplementary information from some of her sources. Unfortunately, however, when she had written the first draft of her thesis, she had copied quotes directly from articles she had *borrowed* from another instructor, without first putting the quotes on cards. (She apparently had not kept up with the three-month schedule and was trying to make up for lost time.) She found herself without the articles, without the note cards, and 800 miles from the LSU library. In short, she ended up doing a lot of unnecessary work, under a lot of unnecessary stress.

The main thing to keep in mind at this stage is not to fight the criticism you get--you must use it to make life easier for your reader.

An Overview

The following outline summarizes the main points in the four stages we have looked at in this chapter.

Stage I: Random Reading (one month)
    1.   read in field
    2.   identify pressing questions in field
    3.   learn major references in field
    4.   keep list of reading (complete bibliographical entries)
    5.   generate idea (at best) or topic (at least)
    6.   ABSTRACT

Chapter 3: Time Management

Stage II: Focussed Reading (one month)
1. identify reading relevant to idea
2. assemble relevant reading
3. read assembled material making marginal notes and highlighting
4. copy usable material onto note cards
    a. one card per quote/observation
    b. include author, year, and page number
    c. include interpretation/relevance
    d. title each card (in red)
5. arrange cards into stacks, according to title
6. arrange stacks
7. arrange cards within stacks
8. CONFERENCE PAPER

Stage III: Write First Draft (two weeks)
1. copy material from cards, including references
2. add transitions and revise organization as necessary
3. add introduction and conclusion
4. revise at word level (be hard on yourself)
5. FIRST DRAFT

Stage IV: Write Final Draft (two weeks)
1. solicit feedback
2. assess feedback
3. delete as necessary (be ruthless)
4. reorganize as necessary (follow head, not heart)
5. supplement as necessary (easy, if II done thoroughly)
6. revise at word level (don't weaken)
7. FINAL DRAFT

In the following chapters we will look more closely at four types of academic products: the abstract, the conference presentation, the response article, and the research article.

Chapter 4: The Abstract

Virtually all professional organizations have at least one convention a year. Six to nine months before the convention, the organizers send out a "call for papers," where they specify the topics that will be covered at the conference and invite members (and sometimes non-members) to submit abstracts for oral presentations. An abstract is essentially an abbreviated version of a paper. It is on the basis of these abstracts that the conference organizers choose presentations--hence the importance of knowing how to write an effective abstract.

The Call for Papers

You can stay informed about upcoming conferences in several ways. First, professional organizations (e.g., the Modern Language Association, the Linguistic Society of America, the American Historical Association, etc.) send their members information about their upcoming conferences; as a member of such an organization, you will receive the information through the mail. Second, professional journals often publish notices of upcoming conferences. Third, if you are affiliated with a department at a university, there is probably a bulletin board where your department head or director of graduate studies posts notices about upcoming conferences.

Figure 4.1 contains the text of a call for papers that appeared in the Winter 1994 issue of *Technical Communication Quarterly*.

Chapter 4: The Abstract

Call for Papers

**Rocky Mountain MLA Section on Technical
and Professional Communications**

**1994 Rocky Mountain Modern Language Association Annual Meeting
Colorado Springs, Colorado
October 27-29, 1994**

Proposals are invited for four permanent and one special session for the 1994 RMMLA Annual Meeting.

1)   Technical Communication in the classroom. (Focus: Addressing Diversity in the Classroom and in the Workplace.)
2)   Technical and Professional Communication in the Workplace.
3)   Theory and Research in Technical and Professional Communication. (Focus: Reading and Using Workplace Writing.)
4)   Forces of Change in Technical and Professional Communication. (Focus: Technical/Professional Communication and Quality.)

Special Session: Beyond the Written Page: Visual Communication and New Technologies. (Possible topics include research in visual communication and other nonverbal communication, hypertext, hypercard, on-screen documentation, new technologies and applications, and other developments "beyond the written page.")

Each presentation will last 15-20 minutes. Speakers must be members of the RMMLA by April 1, 1994.

Send a two-page proposal for a presentation on one of the above topics by March 15, 1994 to

Cezar M. Ornatowski
Department of Rhetoric and Writing Studies
San Diego State University
San Diego, California 92184
(619) 594-6927

Figure 4.1. Focussed Call for Papers

Chapter 4: The Abstract

This is a fairly standard call for papers. The conference is a regional meeting of a large professional organization; within this meeting, five sessions will be devoted to technical and professional communication. The call for papers suggests a focus for each session; respondents whose proposals (i.e., abstracts) fall within this focus are, of course, more likely to be invited to present their papers. The organizer has asked for two-page proposals; in other calls for papers, you might see the abstract length stated in terms of a maximum number of words (e.g., "send a 250-word abstract . . .").

Note also that the proposals are due seven months in advance of the conference itself: by March 15 for an October 27-29 conference. In fact, a lead time of six months to a year between the deadline for abstracts and the conference itself is not uncommon. This allows conference organizers time to read and respond to the proposals and coordinate the variety and number of papers that will be presented. As we will see later in this chapter, this lead time can affect the strategies that you use in preparing your abstract.

By way of comparison, consider another call for papers, shown in Figure 4.2. (This one was posted on a bulletin board by the director of graduate studies in an English department.) While this bears some similarities to the first example we looked at, we can infer several differences between the two conferences. First, note that the deadline for submitting abstracts to the Midlands conference is much closer to the conference itself than that for the Rocky Mountain conference (only two months as opposed to seven months). This suggests that the Midlands conference is probably more informal, operating on a smaller scale, and expecting a smaller response to their call for papers. Otherwise the conference organizer

Chapter 4: The Abstract

CALL FOR PAPERS

EIGHTH ANNUAL

MIDLANDS CONFERENCE ON

LANGUAGE & LITERATURE

MARCH 31-APRIL 1, 1995

HOSTED BY CREIGHTON UNIVERSITY

Papers on any aspect of language, literature (including literature for children and young adults), or linguistics will be acceptable. Presentations must not exceed twenty minutes, allowing for a ten-minute discussion period.

Special sessions include: Irish poet, James Liddy; American Minority Women Writers; Computers as Invention Tool.

The **deadline** for receipt of a two-page abstract is **February 1, 1995.**

We would appreciate your posting this Call for Papers conspicuously; please feel free to duplicate it. Respond to:

Kathleen Collins
Department of English
2500 California Plaza
Creighton University
Omaha, NE 68178
Phone: (402) 280-2822 or (402) 426-3294

Figure 4.2. General Call for Papers

would have left herself more time to coordinate the proposals and organize the resultant sessions. From a proposer's perspective, the Midlands conference is probably the less competitive of the two.

Second, note that, with the exception of the three special sessions, the Midlands conference is accepting papers on an extremely wide range of topics (i.e., "any aspect of language, literature . . . , or linguistics"). This can be both good and bad. On the positive side, it means that practically any topic in an English, foreign language, or linguistics department curriculum stands a chance of being accepted. On the negative side, it also means that the Midlands conference may be uneven in focus and, perhaps, in quality. At best, it will be eclectic. By comparison, only papers on technical communication can be submitted to the Rocky Mountain conference. Therefore, someone interested in this subject has a good chance of hearing some useful ideas at that meeting. Since most academics go to conferences to listen to papers as well as to present them, this is worth keeping in mind when responding to a call for papers.

Preparing the Abstract

As mentioned earlier, an abstract is essentially an abbreviated version of a paper, typically ranging from 100 to 250 words. There are essentially two different types of abstracts. One we might call a TOPIC abstract and the other a THESIS abstract. The former describes the *subject* that the author deals with in the paper, and the latter articulates the *claim* that the author attempts to support in the paper. (TOPIC abstracts are sometimes called "descriptive" or "indicative" abstracts, and THESIS abstracts are sometimes called "summary" or "informative" abstracts.")

Chapter 4: The Abstract

Consider, for example, the following two abstracts of the same paper. (Both are from Manning, 1990: 370; emphasis and labels have been added.)

TOPIC Allergies and low humidity, and bacterial or viral infections are common causes of throat irritation. *This report reviews* the effectiveness of over-the-counter medications in curing, preventing, or relieving discomfort of sore throats. Alternative home treatments are discussed.

THESIS Over-the-counter medications (OTCs) cannot cure or prevent sore throats caused by bacterial or viral infections. Studies show antiseptic mouthwashes have no medicinal advantage over water. *This report recommends* that sore-throat sufferers avoid OTCs, use salt-water gargles and ordinary aspirin for discomfort, and consult a physician if the sore throat persists.

The TOPIC abstract informs the reader only of the subject matter of the paper--sore throats and their treatment. This is suggested by the phrase *This report reviews* . . . . The abstract itself is non-committal concerning the conclusions reached in the paper. In contrast, the THESIS abstract tells the reader not only the subject matter of the paper (sore throats) but also the position that the author takes (sufferers should gargle salt water, take aspirin, and avoid over-the-counter medications). This is suggested by the phrase *This report recommends* . . . .

Manning constructed his examples to illustrate the differences between the two types of abstracts. Now let's consider some examples of abstracts actually appearing in the literature. The following example, taken from the *Newsletter of the American Dialect Society*, describes a paper to be presented at the Society's annual meeting (emphasis added).

Chapter 4: The Abstract

> **New England French in New York State: The French of Cohoes, N.Y.** *Cynthia A. Fox*, State Univ. of New York, Albany. It is estimated that there are 900,000 people of French ancestry in New York State, a large proportion of them descended from the nearly one million French Canadians who left Quebec between 1840 and 1940 seeking better economic conditions. *This paper reports preliminary findings* of field work conducted in Cohoes, N.Y. during the summer of 1991. *It is hypothesized that* relegation of the New York Francos to the periphery of the Franco-American geographical space has contributed to accelerated language loss and placed its membership at the lower end of a Quebec-New England-New York continuum of French language maintenance in North America. (1991: 5)

First, note that this is a THESIS abstract: the phrase *It is hypothesized that . . .* states the claim that the author will attempt to support in her paper. Second, note that this abstract could be turned into a TOPIC abstract by deleting the final sentence. Thus, the abstract would end simply with a description of the subject to be discussed: *This paper reports preliminary findings . . . .*

It should be obvious that a THESIS abstract is more effective than a TOPIC abstract, especially if your purpose is to convince the people putting on a conference to choose your idea for presentation rather than someone else's. It is often the case, however, that you simply don't know exactly what you're going to find or how you're going to present your findings before you do your study. (This is especially true of experimental research.) Moreover, the logistics of submitting abstracts to conferences may force you to write a topic abstract, since some conferences require you to submit an abstract nearly a year in advance. Most participants simply do not have their final thesis worked out this far ahead.

Chapter 4: The Abstract

As an illustration, consider the following two abstracts, both by Riley, of essentially the same piece of work. The first was written *before* the research was carried out, as the basis for a conference presentation. The second was written *after* the research was done, as a summary accompanying a published article. (Boldface has been added.)

BEFORE

BACKGROUND

For several decades, analysts have held two opposing views toward the passive voice in scientific writing. Most have advised avoiding the passive whenever possible. Those supporting this view argue (1) that passive voice (e.g., *Six samples were examined by the team*) is inherently longer and thus "wordier" than active voice (e.g., *The team examined six samples*), and (2) that the passive allows agent deletion (as in *Six samples were examined*) and thus may obscure who or what performed the action. More recently, however, passive voice has been defended by others who argue that (1) it may improve the flow between old and new information, and (2) agent deletion is appropriate when the agent's identity is unknown or unimportant.

PURPOSE

Previous analyses have focused on isolated passive sentences or, at most, paragraph-length passages of discourse. Further, they have been prescriptive rather than descriptive (i.e., making claims in advance about how scientists *should* write, rather than examining how scientists actually *do* write). To avoid these limitations, the proposed study will examine the use of passive voice in 10 scientific articles. **The hypothesis to be tested is that the active/passive ratio changes systematically as a function of the writer's**

Chapter 4: The Abstract

	changing role within an extended piece of scientific discourse.
METHODOLOGY	The works to be studied are articles reporting experimental studies in speech-language pathology from the *Journal of Speech and Hearing Disorders*. Each article displays a uniform division into four sections: Introduction, Methodology, Results, and Conclusion. These sections, in turn, correspond to different authorial roles: as a critic of previous work (in the Introduction, which typically reviews prior research); as a presenter of new data (in the sections on Methodology and Results); and as an interpreter of data and advocate of a thesis (in the Conclusion). From a rhetorical perspective, these divisions reflect a movement from argumentation (in the Introduction) to exposition (in the sections on Methodology and Results) and back to argumentation (in the Conclusion).
ANTICIPATED RESULTS	Researchers in scientific writing have called for more substantive research in order to test and modify current assumptions about their subject. To this end, the proposed study will examine how writers from one scientific community use specific linguistic strategies (i.e., active and passive voice) for specific rhetorical purposes. Such research, in turn, has implications for both the theory and pedagogy of scientific writing.

AFTER

BACKGROUND & PURPOSE	As analysts of scientific writing begin to modify their stance against the passive voice and explore the complexities of its use, more research is needed on the rhetorical functions it serves in scientific writing. An analysis of twelve articles reporting experimental studies in speech-language pathology revealed consistently higher percentages
METHODOLOGY	

45

Chapter 4: The Abstract

RESULTS of passive structures in the Method and Results sections. **These findings suggest that *passive structures* are more appropriate for *expository* purposes, in those sections where the author's rhetorical role is to describe procedures and present data. In contrast, *active structures* are more appropriate for *argumentative* purposes, in those sections where the author is criticizing previous research or advocating a new thesis.** (1991: 239)

The first thing to note about these abstracts is their components: they both are organized in terms of BACKGROUND, PURPOSE, METHODOLOGY, and RESULTS. The second thing to note is that they are both THESIS abstracts. (The thesis has been boldfaced in both examples.) The only difference is that the thesis is quite *general* in the first version but very *specific* in the second. This difference, of course, reflects the fact that the author knew less before doing the study than after doing it.

The "After" example also illustrates another use of the abstract, namely as a summary that accompanies a published article. Typically an abstract written for this purpose appears immediately after the title of the article but before the text of the article begins. Sometimes it appears in the table of contents of the journal. This type of abstract is quite common in the sciences and social sciences, and is starting to make its way into the humanities as well. For example, *PMLA*, the journal of the Modern Language Association, publishes abstracts in its table of contents. For obvious reasons, such summaries are always thesis abstracts.

Before closing this chapter on abstracts, we want to mention the role of references in abstracts. Although abstracts

Chapter 4: The Abstract

need not contain references, their inclusion can add weight to an abstract submitted as the basis for a conference presentation. That is, references may help convince the conference organizers that the prospective participant has already begun his or her research and actually will have a well-conceived argument to present. Consider the following abstract, which we submitted to a recent panel sponsored by the Association of Teachers of Technical Writing.

>   Ethics, Politics, and Indirectness
>
> Analyses of unethical communication have typically focused on **intentional** attempts to mislead the reader. For examples, analysts have pointed out that indirectness strategies--most notably indirect speech acts and implicature--can be manipulated to deceive the reader. For example, in the "Sharon G." case discussed by Buchholz (1989), a consultant tells a prospective client that she cannot begin working with his company until late summer, when she finishes work as a freelance advisor under contract to the Public Affairs Office at the Harvard Business School. Although the consultant does not lie, she omits significant information: "that her work with Harvard is very low level, does not relate significantly to [the client's] company, and has come to her . . . through the machinations of her fiance." Buchholz describes the consultant's intent as "deviously self-serving, for she wants the prospective client to hear `Harvard B-School' in all its attendant glory" (p. 67). Grice's theory of implicature, specifically the Maxim of Quantity, provides an elegant explanation of why the consultant's communication in unethical. Similarly, in the "Rail Car Rhetoric" case discussed by Walzer (1989), implicature is used to intentionally mislead a reader about a product's performance and safety.
>
> In practice, the ethics and politics of indirectness lead to a more complex and commonplace problem than has been previously noted. Specifically, well-meaning writers may run the risk of **unintentionally** misleading the reader by using indirectness strategies for perfectly legitimate purposes: to save face, show deference, or mitigate bad news. For example, both the Three Mile Island and

Chapter 4: The Abstract

Challenger incidents can be attributed in part to extremely indirect communication which led, in turn to misunderstandings about responsibility and authority (Herndl et al. 1991; Winsor 1998). Similarly, a recent lawsuit won against a tampon manufacturer concerned a package insert that relied too heavily on indirectness strategies (Shuy 1990). The writer of the insert used indirect, rather than direct, speech acts to alert the consumer to the dangers of toxic shock syndrome. Additionally, the insert relied heavily on implicature to make connections between tampon use and toxic shock syndrome, rather than stating these connections explicitly.

In none of these three cases, however, is there evidence of an intent to deceive. Instead, the use of indirectness originates from a desire to show deference to someone higher in the corporate structure or to mitigate unpleasant information. Ironically, then, an attempt to play by the rules of corporate politics and public relations is often the catalyst for inadvertently misleading communication. The inappropriate use of indirectness may also reflect problems in audience analysis: a writer may mistakenly assume that a reader has the requisite background to draw an inference from information given in the text.

Although indirectness strategies carry the potential to mislead, they themselves are neither inherently ethical nor unethical. Consequently, it would be misguided to encourage writers to avoid indirectness strategies altogether. For one thing, such strategies remain a powerful tool for dealing with sensitive rhetorical situations (Riley 1988a, 1988b). Moreover, indirectness strategies are part of everyone's unconscious linguistic repertoire; therefore, it makes no more sense to speak of eliminating indirectness than, say, of eliminating nouns. Instead, we encourage more analysis of the circumstances under which writers use indirectness and of how readers interpret (and misinterpret) indirect communication.

References

Buchholz, W. J. (1989). "Deciphering Professional Codes of Ethics." *IEEE Transactions on Professional Communication 32*, 62-68.

Herndl, C. G., B. A. Fennell, and C. R. Miller (1991). "Understanding Failures in Organizational Discourse: The Accident at Three Mile Island and the Shuttle Challenger

Disaster," in *Textual Dynamics of the Professions*, ed. C. Bazerman and J. Paradis (Madison: U. of Wisconsin Press), 279-305.

Riley, K. (1988a). "Speech Act Theory and Degrees of Directness in Professional Writing," *The Technical Writing Teacher 15*, 1-29.

Riley, K. (1988b). "Conversational Implicature and Unstated Meaning in Professional Communication," *The Technical Writing Teacher 15*, 94-104.

Shuy, R. (1990). "Warning Labels: Language, Law, and Comprehensibility," *American Speech 65*, 291-303.

Walzer, A. E. (1989). "The Ethics of False Implicature in Technical and Professional Writing Courses," *Journal of Technical Writing and Communication 19*, 149-160.

Winsor, D. A. (1988). "Communication Failures Contributing to the Challenger Accident: An Example for Technical Communicators," *IEEE Transactions on Professional Communication 31*, 101-107.

In this case, abstracts had to be limited to two pages, so we used the extra space to augment the abstract with references.

In sum, the challenge of an abstract is to be convincing and lucid in a severely restricted space. Our best advice is to: (1) aim for a THESIS abstract (rather than a TOPIC abstract); (2) make your thesis as specific as you can; and (3) include references if space allows.

Chapter 5: The Conference Presentation

In the previous chapter we suggested ways to compose an abstract for a conference presentation. In this chapter we want to look more closely at the role of conference papers and suggest some ways to deliver an oral presentation effectively.

The Role of Conference Papers

Conference papers are especially important to those just beginning their careers. For one thing, they provide you with visibility. For example, you may be giving a paper at a conference where you are also interviewing for jobs. If so, the audience may include members of a hiring committee or prospective colleagues. In this case, the conference paper represents an opportunity for you to demonstrate, indirectly, your scholarship and teaching skills. (Even if you are not on the job market when you are giving a conference presentation, members of the audience may remember you later on--for better or for worse.)

Second, most academic departments encourage and reward participation at conferences, since they increase the university's visibility. If you are a tenure-track faculty member, you probably have some allotment of travel money from your department. (Some graduate programs also have funds available for graduate student travel.) However, many departments pay for travel to conferences only if the faculty member is presenting a paper or chairing a session. Thus,

Chapter 5: The Conference Presentation

participating in the conference may be the only way you can get the university to pay your way.

Third, a conference presentation gives you a chance not only to get your ideas into the public forum but also to obtain feedback from your colleagues. Typically, the conference paper represents a look at your work in progress--for example, a hypothesis that has been confirmed by your initial research, but has not yet been presented in print. (In fact, some conferences expressly forbid you from presenting a paper based on a published article.) The question-and-answer period following your presentation will give you some sense of what points in your argument you need to clarify or bolster.

While conference papers are valuable for these reasons, we would like to add a word of caution about overdoing conference papers, especially early in your career. We have seen more than one colleague at the assistant professor level get carried away with "conference fever," traveling to as many as eight or nine conferences a year, giving presentation after presentation, but never getting any of it into print. Parker had a colleague like this who, after being turned down for early promotion and tenure, became bitter and quit academics altogether. Put simply, it's easier to write a one-page abstract and get it accepted for a conference than it is to write a 20-page article and get it accepted by a journal. The fact is, though, that at evaluation time (e.g., when a decision about hiring, tenure, or promotion is being made), the journal article carries far more weight. No one has ever been hired, tenured, or promoted on the basis of conference presentations alone. For this reason, we would advise beginning academics to limit

Chapter 5: The Conference Presentation

themselves to one or two conferences a year. Focus instead on following through on your ideas and getting them into print.

Preparing an Effective Conference Paper

There are three fundamental rules for making a successful oral presentation: (1) speak extemporaneously (i.e., don't read); (2) stay within your time limit; and (3) use a visual aid. Any deviation from this advice can make your audience very unhappy and they, in turn, can make you very unhappy. Let's consider these points one at a time.

Extemporaneous Speaking. The most effective delivery style for a conference paper is to give your presentation *extemporaneously*. By an extemporaneous style, we mean one in which the exact wording of each sentence is not set in advance. In other words, you are not reading from a prepared text. On the other hand, the sequence of ideas and the key phrases associated with each idea are worked out beforehand. The best way to achieve this style is to prepare an outline or visual to go along with your talk and then use the outline or visual itself as a prompt. (More on this later.)

The reason for using an extemporaneous style has to do with the conference situation. Conferences usually last two or three days and consist of four to six sessions a day; each session, in turn, lasts for about one-and-a-half to two hours and consists of three or four papers--that's as many as 36 hours of oral presentations that an audience listens to in just a few days. Moreover, most conference papers are somewhat technical. That is, they are more likely to have titles like "Linguistics,

Chapter 5: The Conference Presentation

Technical Writing, and Generalized Phrase Structure Grammar" than "How to Talk Minnesotan." Thus, listening to as many as 72 people go to the front of an auditorium and *read* academic papers over a three-day period would be a lot like having a math instructor come to class and *read* from *College Algebra* for an hour three times a week for fifteen straight weeks.

Unfortunately, most people giving oral presentations at a professional conference prepare a paper for publication and simply *read* it to the audience. There is something about reading, however, that puts people to sleep. (Note that parents *read* to their children to help them go to sleep.) Some presenters think it's all right to read from a script if they do it with a "lively" or "dramatic" tone of voice, meant to give the impression that they are speaking extemporaneously. However, this does not avoid two problems inherent in reading from a text: one, a lack of eye contact; and two, a reliance on word choice, sentence structure, and sentence length that still reflect the written word rather than unselfconscious speech.

It's interesting to speculate on why many people feel compelled to stand up and *read* a 20-30 minute monologue, when good sense would dictate otherwise. Apparently, they fear being struck dumb by stage fright. The word-for-word script that they carry with them seems to serve as a security blanket. A script can be read unconsciously long after the mind blanks out; an extemporaneous talk, on the other hand, requires control of conscious thought.

As an illustration of how resistant people are to speaking extemporaneously, consider this anecdote. Several

Chapter 5: The Conference Presentation

years ago, Parker organized a session on Language Theory for the Modern Language Association's annual convention. Once he had chosen the papers to be presented, he wrote to each speaker and, among other things, instructed them explicitly *not to read their papers*. When the conference actually occurred, the co-authors of one paper not only read it word-for-word from a prepared text, but *alternated* paragraphs--that is, one would read a paragraph while the other one sat, and then the other would jump up and read while the first one sat. It was indeed a stunning performance.

Time Limit. Just as important as using an extemporaneous style is staying within your time limit. Simply put, going over your time limit is extremely rude, both to your audience and to the other speakers on the panel. Speakers at conferences are generally given between 15 and 30 minutes for their presentation. This includes being introduced by the chairperson, making the presentation itself, and answering questions from the audience. This means that, if you're given a 25-minute allotment, you have to reserve five minutes for the introduction and general time-wasting and five minutes for questions; this leaves 15 minutes for your talk.

Unfortunately, you can't assume that the session chair will enforce a time limit on any of the speakers, including you. Too often, there is no polite way for a session chair to stop another speaker who is exceeding his or her time limit. Therefore, you should be prepared to monitor your own speaking time and to compensate for other speakers who take too much time. This means you have to *practice*. The best way to do this is ask two or three of your colleagues (e.g., faculty or classmates) to serve as an audience while you run

Chapter 5: The Conference Presentation

through your presentation. Their job is not only to time you (i.e., make sure you stay within your 15 minutes) but also to critique your presentation (e.g., "You try to make too many points; you need an example here; you need a visual there").

The fundamental fact to keep in mind throughout this process is that a conference presentation is an entirely different *genre* from a paper you send to a journal. (It's easy to get these two things confused since academics often do both with the same idea.) The most significant difference is *time*. In a journal article, time is not a factor. Readers can cover it at their own pace. They can re-read it or go back and refer to specific sections. A conference paper is, however, severely constrained by time. Consequently, no one expects you to argue your case or document each point exhaustively. Rather, in an oral presentation all you can do is outline the general problem, propose a general solution, and give one or two examples of each. It's the failure to understand and accept the difference between a journal article and a conference presentation that causes so many academics to embarrass themselves by trying to pack a two-hour journal article, complete with footnotes and references, into a 15-minute oral presentation.

Here's an illustration. A number of years ago, Parker was one of three speakers on a panel at the annual meeting of the American Dialect Society. The session was scheduled for an hour and 15 minutes, giving each speaker 25 minutes. The first speaker was introduced, walked to the stage, gave his presentation in 15 minutes, and answered questions. The second speaker (Parker) did the same. Then came the third speaker. When he was introduced he got up from where he

Chapter 5: The Conference Presentation

was sitting in the back of the auditorium and started handing out copies of his visual to the audience. (Note that he was wasting his own time. He should have done this *before* the session started or had someone else hand out the visual for him.) The visual itself resembled the phone book of a small city, maybe Des Moines; it felt like it was 50 pages long. Moreover, it was filled with page after page of fine phonetic transcription--a real cure for insomnia.

When the third speaker took the stage, he pulled out what appeared to be another phone book, this time for Manhattan, and began to read. As the time passed, the session chair slipped pieces of paper onto the podium where the speaker could see them: "10 minutes left," "5 minutes left," "2 minutes left," "Time's up," and so forth. Each time she put one of these messages in front of the speaker, he would stop reading, flip ahead a handful of pages in his text, and begin reading again--randomly. After he'd been going on for 35 minutes--10 minutes over his allotted time--the session chair stood up, shouldered him out of the way, grabbed the microphone, and said, "Guess that'll just have to wait till next year."

The moral of the story is to treat the audience with the same consideration that you yourself would like to be afforded. We once heard a speaker at a conference announce, as she took the podium, "I hope you won't mind if I go over my time limit a little, because I know you're just as interested in this subject as I am." The fact is we *do* mind.

Visual Aids. Any oral presentation should be augmented by some sort of visual aid. (Even children are

56

Chapter 5: The Conference Presentation

encouraged to use them; note that their classroom activity is called "*Show* and tell," not just "Tell.") The primary function of a visual aid is to compensate for the fact that you have only a few minutes to make your point. (Note that in the 1992 election campaign, Clinton adopted Ross Perot's strategy of using charts in explaining his budget on television.)

Visual aids include slides, overheads, photocopied handouts, and even the use of a blackboard. The two most commonly used visual aids, at least in the humanities, are handouts and overheads. The advantage of a handout is that the audience has something to take home with them. The disadvantage is that the audience may be attending to one part of the handout while you are trying to focus their attention on another part. On the other hand, overheads allow you to control what the audience sees at any point during your talk. The disadvantage is that they have nothing to take with them for reference later on. Our own preference is for the use of an overhead; but since photocopying is available virtually everywhere, we will restrict the following discussion to handouts. (Most of what we have to say is, of course, applicable to any type of visual.)

Good handouts have three properties: they are (1) short, (2) simple, and (3) dependent upon interpretation. By *short*, we mean that they should be no more than one single sheet of 8½" x 11" paper. This allows you to fit two pages of information on one sheet: one page photocopied onto the front of the sheet and one onto the back. If necessary, you can put four pages onto one sheet by reducing each page by 50% and photocopying two pages onto the front and two onto the back. (This latter method should never be used as a substitute for

Chapter 5: The Conference Presentation

editing. If you can't cover information in 15 minutes, reducing your visual aid won't help.) A single-sheet handout makes you look like you're in control of your subject; a four-sheet handout, even if it contains exactly the same information, makes you look like you're at the mercy of it.

By *simple*, we mean uncluttered; your audience should be able to grasp your point from a glance at the handout. Any visual that requires paper and pencil analysis (or a magnifying glass) is not simple. We'll try to illustrate this with the following two figures (courtesy of Alan Manning). Figure 5.1 shows the relationship between the lens opening of a camera and its shutter speed. Figure 5.2 illustrates the differences and similarities among the interrogative pronouns in English.

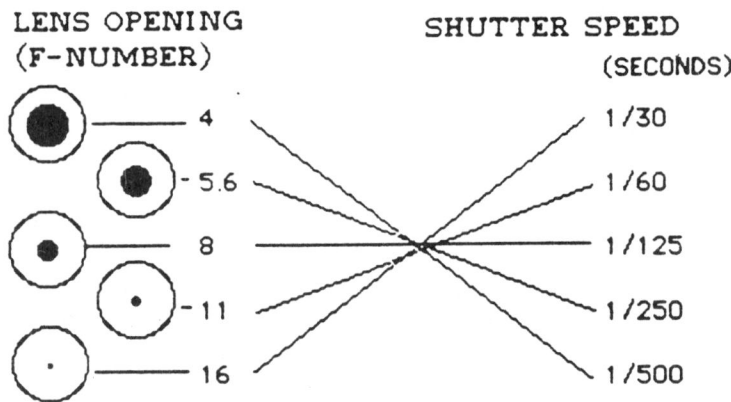

Figure 5.1. Relation of Lens Opening to Shutter Speed

Chapter 5: The Conference Presentation

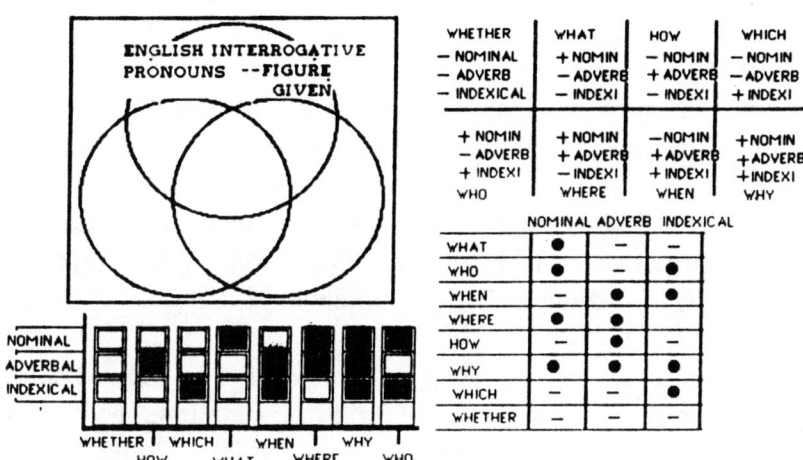

Figure 5.2. Properties of Interrogative Pronouns

Figure 5.1 is simple. It's clear, even from a glance, that Figure 5.1 is designed to illustrate a single point--the relation between lens opening and shutter speed; it contains a column of values for each one and lines connecting them. Figure 5.2, however, is not simple. It's not clear if it's one figure or four. It simply contains too many details for a viewer to process at a glance. Are the overlapping circles related to the rest of the figure? Do the black squares serve the same functions as the black dots? Are the minus signs in the upper right equivalent to the dashes in the lower right? And so on.

Chapter 5: The Conference Presentation

The third property of a good handout, *dependent upon interpretation*, means that it should not make complete sense without some oral interpretation by the speaker. In other words, the audience should not be able to sit there and *read* the handout as though it were a newspaper article. If the handout is fully interpretable on its own, then the audience will not attend to the speaker. The best way to insure that the audience is not distracted by your handout is to make sure it contains no prose. That is, it may contain figures and tables; it may contain quotations, examples, and phrases; but it should contain no interpretation. It is the speaker's job to interpret the material in the handout for the audience.

The best way to illustrate this point is to look at some real handouts actually used in oral presentations before an audience. First, consider the handout entitled "Cohesion and Coherence" in Figure 5.3.

Note that this handout is short: the entire handout can fit on one side of one sheet of paper. Note, too, that it is simple: it has four parts (note the Roman numerals down the left-hand side), and each part consists of at most two sample sentences or two figures. (The numerals and letters, by the way, allow the speaker to refer to items in a way that the audience can easily identify. For example, she can direct the audience to "Example B1 under Section III instead of "the next example" or "the example toward the bottom.") Moreover, note that the handout is completely dependent on interpretation: there is not a single sentence on this page other than the sample sentences. In other words, there is nothing for the audience to sit and read while the speaker is talking. They can *look at* the

Chapter 5: The Conference Presentation

COHESION AND COHERENCE
Kim Sydow Campbell

I. A Semantic Theory of Cohesion (Halliday & Hasan [1976])

    A. <u>Jim's dog died. He loved that animal.</u>
    B. <u>Veni, Vidi, Vici!</u>

II. A Perceptual Theory of Cohesion

    A.

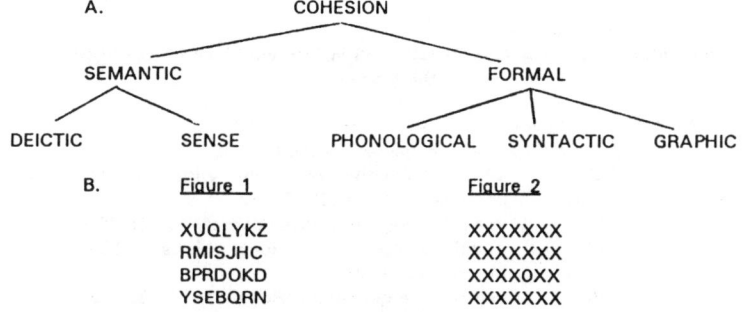

    B.   <u>Figure 1</u>   <u>Figure 2</u>

```
        XUQLYKZ        XXXXXXX
        RMISJHC        XXXXXXX
        BPRDOKD        XXXXOXX
        YSEBQRN        XXXXXXX
```

    Formal Repetition (Phonological): <u>Veni</u>, <u>Vidi</u> & <u>Vici</u> (alliteration)
    Semantic Repetition (Sense): <u>dog</u> & <u>animal</u> [+alive/-human]

III. A Semantic/Pragmatic Theory of Coherence

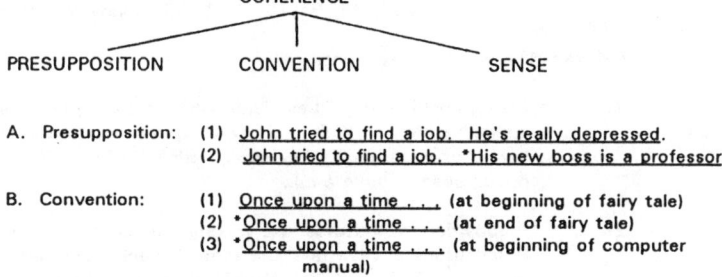

    A. Presupposition: (1) <u>John tried to find a job. He's really depressed</u>.
                            (2) <u>John tried to find a job. *His new boss is a professor</u>.

    B. Convention: (1) <u>Once upon a time . . .</u> (at beginning of fairy tale)
                            (2) *<u>Once upon a time . . .</u> (at end of fairy tale)
                            (3) *<u>Once upon a time . . .</u> (at beginning of computer manual)

IV. Confusion Between COHESION & COHERENCE

	(Repetition) COHESION	(Expectation) COHERENCE
(1) <u>Jim's pet died. He loved that dog</u>.	[+alive/-human]	prototype
(2) <u>turtle</u>	[+alive/-human]	extension
(3) <u>roach</u>	[+alive/-human]	not in extension

Figure 5.3. Cohesion and Coherence

Chapter 5: The Conference Presentation

handout, but they can't *read* it. They are dependent upon the speaker to interpret it for them.

In contrast, consider the handout entitled "Linguistics and the Art of Questioning" in Figure 5.4.

Linguistics and the Art of Questioning in Interviews and Interrogation
Bill Harrell

I. Problem: Unprincipled advice
    1. Anecdotal wisdom gained by experience
        a) avoid suggestive questions with mentally defective persons (Bristow, 1958: 67)
        b) avoid leading questions (Gerber, 1962: 296)
        c) avoid complex questions (Royal, 1976: 34-35; MacHovec, 1989: 94)
        d) use precise questions (Royal, 1976: 32-33)
        e) have "the gift of gab" (Firth, 1975: 1507)

    2. Good practical advice but no theory
        a) ask what, when, where, why, how, who, which (Rapp, 1987: 20; Royal, 1976: 35; MacHovec, 1989: 107)
        b) ask questions as if answers already known (Inbau, 1962: 99; Royal, 1976: 33; Zulawski, 1992: 131)

II. Relevant Linguistics: Presupposition

    1. Presupposition describes "any kind of background assumption against which an action, theory, expression, or utterance makes sense or is rational" (Levinson, 1983: 168). "My car is blue" presupposes *I have a car.*

    2. Proposition constitutes the meaningful content of a sentence. Propositions always take the form of declarative sentences.
        a) "Did John kick Mary?" expresses the proposition *John kicked Mary* but does not presuppose that proposition.
        b) "When did John kick Mary?" expresses same proposition and also presupposes it.

    3. Presupposition Triggers--entire classes of words and structures that convey presuppositions
        a) wh-words: see section I.2.a above
        b) wh-words presuppose proposition of which they are a part (Levinson, 1983: 184)

Chapter 5: The Conference Presentation

III. Solution: Presupposition Triggers

    1. Approaches suggested in manuals with selective analysis of data
- a. <u>Bluff</u>: "**When** did you get out?" rather than "Have you even been in jail?" (Bristow, 1958: 69). "When did you get out?" expresses the proposition 'you got out.' The presupposition is *you were in*.
- b. <u>Prompting</u>: "**What** did you do then?" (Rapp, 1987:21) presupposes *you did something then*.
   <u>Sympathy</u>: "**What** will your family think?" (Rapp, 1987: 79) presupposes *your family will think something*
   <u>Rapport</u>: "**What** do your friends call you?" (Rapp, 1987: 211)
- c. <u>Direct Approach</u>: "**Where** is the money now?" (Aubry, 1972: 190)
- d. <u>Baiting</u>: "**How** long have you known John Jones?" rather than "Do you know John Jones?" (Inbau, 1986: 71)
   <u>Off the Record</u>: "**How** did you get away with it so long?" (Rapp, 1987: 81) presupposes *you got away with it so long*.
- e. <u>Emotional Hate Approach</u>: "**Why** do you think they allowed you to be captured?" (Army Field Manual 34-52, 1992: 3-15) presupposes *you do think that they allowed you to be captured*.

    2. Overview of Presupposition Triggers and Their Inclusion in Questioning Approaches

        The names of methods or approaches may vary but most incorporate presupposition triggers, e.g., wh-words. The questioner intuitively chooses the proposition and the appropriate wh-word question to fit the approach he wishes to use.

Figure 5.4. Linguistics and the Art of Questioning

Like the handout on cohesion and coherence, this one is short: two pages photocopied onto the front and back of one sheet of paper. Likewise, it is relatively simple: it has three major sections, each with an informative heading. On the other hand, it contains too much prose; it invites the audience to *read* rather than listen. Note, for example, the prose definitions in part II of "presupposition" and "proposition." Likewise, note the very last item, III.2. The heading is too long ("Overview

Chapter 5: The Conference Presentation

of Presupposition Triggers and their Inclusion in Questioning Approaches"), and it is followed by a *paragraph*--the paragraph has only two sentences, but it's a paragraph nonetheless. The main flaw in this handout is the author's attempt to *summarize* the written version of his paper. (Note, for example, the ubiquitous references.) An oral presentation is not a summary of a paper, rather it is an *advertisement* for the written product. It is designed to persuade the audience that if they take the time to read the paper, it will be worth their while.

Before leaving the subject of visual aids, we want to say a few words about some of the logistical details associated with them. If you plan to use an overhead projector, make sure that your session chair knows this well in advance (i.e., as soon as your paper is accepted). When you arrive at the conference, double-check the room where your session is scheduled and make sure the overhead projector and screen have been placed in there. If you plan to distribute a handout, be sure to have the copies made before you get to the conference--don't rely on finding a photocopying service the day before you have to give a paper in an unfamiliar city. Before your session begins, arrange to have the handout distributed by someone else (such as the session chair or a colleague in the audience). This way, you can begin your presentation smoothly and on time, without worrying about passing out the handouts.

We have tried to make two basic points in this chapter. First, a conference presentation is a means to an end (i.e., publication), not an end in itself. Second, an oral presentation is a different genre from a research paper; thus, simply reading an article aloud is inadequate.

Chapter 6: The Response Article

After presenting your work orally at a conference, the next step in the process is to turn it into an article for publication in a professional journal. We distinguish between two types of article: the full-blown research paper and the response article. The latter, quite simply, is a paper written in response to a single published article. The response is typically both a criticism and an expansion of the original article.

A response article has two major attractions for a novice writer. First, a response is generally easier to research than an original article. This is because you don't need to synthesize the literature on your subject; at most, you'll have to summarize the article which serves as stimulus to yours. Second, a response article is generally easier to get accepted for publication than a research article. This is because journal editors usually feel obliged to publish a *legitimate* criticism of an article they've already published.

On the other hand, a response article has several liabilities. First, a response is generally considered a somewhat less prestigious publication than an original research paper. The reason for this is obvious: the *other person* had the idea; you're just amending it. Second, a response article has to be written soon after the publication of the original article. As the original paper loses currency with time, so does any interest in your response to it. (Keep in mind that it can take three months to write a response, another three to six months for it to be refereed, and another six to twelve months in production before

Chapter 6: The Response Article

it is actually published. Thus, you may be looking at one to two years between the time you read an article and your response appears in print, *and that's if all goes well*.) Third, a response article is normally of interest only to the journal that published the original article. The editor of any other journal would probably return your paper with the comment: "Why don't you send this response to the journal that published the original article?"

With these points in mind, let's look at some ways to organize and develop a response article.

Organization

Response articles generally follow a recognizable pattern. First, since the author of the response cannot assume that the readers will have read the original article, some summary of the original argument needs to be provided. In other words, the response article needs to be self-contained. Second, the author of the response should acknowledge any positive aspects of the original article or points the author agrees with. After all, if you're going to criticize an article, you should have the self-confidence to give credit where it is due. Third, the response should identify those points which the writer believes have a better (or at least an alternative) explanation or which need more expansion. Then the author of the response provides his or her own contribution.

The best way to illustrate the structure of a response article is to take a look at the actual introductions to a few. Consider, for example, the following introduction to an article

Chapter 6: The Response Article

entitled "Pragmatics and Technical Communication: Some Further Considerations" by Riley.

> In two recent papers in *The Technical Writing Teacher*, Haselkorn (1983, 1984) argues that "The boundaries of technical writing can be defined using concepts from formal linguistics" (1983: 26). More specifically, Haselkorn recommends that the study of syntax and semantics should be limited to the introductory composition course (1983: 29), and that technical writing should focus on "the study and teaching of pragmatic conventions of structure and meaning encountered by people working in technical contexts" (1983:26).
>
> My purpose is to discuss several significant problems with Haselkorn's representation of pragmatics, and consequently with the applicability of his claims to technical writing theory and pedagogy. *First*, Haselkorn represents pragmatics as a domain whose definition is commonly agreed-upon within linguistic theory. In reality, however, a number of diverse views exist about how pragmatics should be defined. *Second*, Haselkorn limits pragmatics to "much larger units" than the sentence (1983: 28) (although how much larger these units need to be is not specified). However, if we look at some specific cases, we find that quite complex pragmatic phenomena arise at the level of the sentence and even at the level of the word. A *third*, related problem is that Haselkorn represents pragmatics as a linguistic domain with discrete boundaries separating it from syntax and semantics. Again, however, if we look at some phenomena that are generally considered to be pragmatic, we find that they cannot be neatly separated from syntax--and, indeed, may be hard to separate from domains such as psycholinguistics and sociolinguistics. (1986: 160; emphasis added)

There are two things to note about this introduction. In the first paragraph, the author summarizes, in very general terms, the article she is critiquing. This serves as a frame of reference and enables the reader to understand Riley's article without necessarily having to read Haselkorn's original. (Note, too, that

Chapter 6: The Response Article

she uses Haselkorn's own words, where possible.) In the second paragraph, the author goes on to enumerate three problems with Haselkorn's articles. Note that in each case she first states Haselkorn's claim and then her objection to it:

HASELKORN	RILEY
1. Pragmatics has one agreed-upon definition.	1. Pragmatics has numerous definitions.
2. Pragmatics deals only with units of discourse larger than a sentence.	2. Pragmatics deals with sentences and words.
3. Pragmatics is separate from syntax.	3. Pragmatics and syntax overlap.

By clearly articulating Haselkorn's claims and her objections in the introduction, Riley was easily able to write an 11-page paper expanding on each of these objections in turn.

Tone

The effect of tone, especially in a response article, cannot be overestimated. Consider the introduction to a response article: "Reflexives Revisited" by P. K. Saha.

> There are *valuable insights* in "Untriggered Reflexive Pronouns in English" .... For example, the notion of removing untriggered reflexive forms in coordinate structures from the list of reflexives and viewing them as "alternative forms for ordinary pronouns" (54) is *helpful* in that it makes the field of true reflexives

Chapter 6: The Response Article

> less cluttered. . . . The article also *breaks new ground* by attempting to set up a hierarchy of acceptability in relation to untriggered reflexives (63).
>
> Alongside these insights, however, there are some problems in the article that seem to call for reexamination of the issues involved. . . . (1993: 319; emphasis added)

What's noteworthy about this introduction is that the author attempts to say what he can that's positive about the original article before he criticizes it. Note that he says the article contains "valuable insights," "is "helpful," and "breaks new ground." This is an effective strategy. It not only makes the author appear unbiased to the editor and referees, it also makes the criticism less offensive to the authors of the original article.

If you can't be positive, at least strive for neutrality. Consider, for example, the tone of a response by Ferguson and Parker (1990) to an article by R. A. Harris (1988). Their introduction follows.

> In a recent paper, "Linguistics, Technical Writing, and Generalized Phrase Structure Grammar," R. A. Harris asserts that "linguistics can be of use to you as a technical writer, and particularly as a technical writing teacher" (p. 228). Harris also claims that since Transformational Grammar (TG) "is largely obsolete" (p. 228), "the best new grammatical model . . . is Generalized Phrase Structure Grammar [GPSG]" (p. 228). Finally, Harris argues for "GPSG's pedagogical advantages" over TG (pp. 233-234).
>
> We agree completely with Harris that linguistics is useful for solving many of the problems encountered in teaching and analyzing technical writing. In fact, a number of recent articles have used linguistic theory to offer insight into seemingly intractable problems

Chapter 6: The Response Article

> encountered in teaching and analyzing technical writing: for example,
> . . . .
>
> However, we think that Harris is not as effective as he could be in arguing his case. On the one hand, his exposition introduces unnecessary and often irrelevant detail, especially when he attempts to articulate fine-grained distinctions between GPSG and TG. In fact, any theoretical differences between GPSG and TG are completely irrelevant to the applications of linguistics to technical writing that he mentions (passives, *yes/no*-questions, extraposition, and given/new information). On the other hand, Harris fails to exploit the full potential of the linguistic principles he does cover. For example, even though he spends most of his paper discussing the passive construction, in his section on "Applications to Technical Writing" he mentions only that many students might improve if they were exposed to the passive "metarule" as formulated in GPSG. In fact, the passive construction plays an important discourse function with respect to both thematic roles and given/new information.
>
> In short, we feel that Harris' paper is emblematic of the misguided attempts to apply linguistics to writing that date back to the 1960s. On the one hand, he confronts the reader (a technical writing specialist) with an overwhelming amount of unnecessary linguistic formalism and arcana. From this perspective, Harris tells the reader TOO MUCH. On the other hand, he fails to show in sufficient detail how the theory can be applied to concrete problems in technical writing. From this perspective, Harris tell the writer TOO LITTLE. Our purpose, then, will be, first, to go over some of the fundamental flaws in Harris' presentation and, second, to use the passive construction to illustrate how linguistics can be used to advantage by technical writing teachers and researchers. (1990: 357-358).

The thing to notice about this introduction is the fact that, even though it is critical of Harris, it is detached and unemotional.

In 1992 Harris responded to Ferguson and Parker's criticism. To see the negative effects of tone, consider the

Chapter 6: The Response Article

following remarks from the introductory and concluding paragraphs of Harris's response paper.

> Ferguson and Parker's recent *attack* on an earlier paper of mine calls for a few brief comments, although I'm very surprised that I had to wait for its publication to see their criticisms. *Scholarly courtesy* should have led them, minimally, to send me a preprint. *Discourtesy*, however, is the least of their *scholarly transgressions*. In their search for a *Bogey Man* against which to highlight the virtues of their own `linguistic' scheme, they completely distort my original paper. . . .
>
> But I will leave it to readers of both articles to decide what might be useful to them in each, and leave the *mean-spirited, school-yardish, my-approach-can-beat-up-your-approach* argumentation to Ferguson and Parker. (1992: 53, 56; emphasis added)

What is most remarkable about Harris's response is not its content but its tone. In particular, note the emotional nature of his rhetoric. According to Harris, Ferguson and Parker "attack" him; they lack "scholarly courtesy"; they commit "scholarly transgressions"; they "search for a Bogey Man"; and their style of argumentation is "mean-spirited, school-yardish, my-approach-can-beat-up-your-approach." The personal and defensive tone of Harris' response is inappropriate. In fact, we think that the editor of *Journal of Technical Writing and Communication*, where the interchange was published, did Harris a real disservice by printing his reply.

In sum, there are two principles that guide a well-written response article: (1) it should be self-contained; that is, the reader should be able to assess your criticisms without necessarily having to read the original paper; and (2) the response should be impersonal and unemotional.

Chapter 7: The Research Article

So far we have looked at four forms of academic discourse: the book review, the abstract, the conference paper, and the response article. At this point we will turn to the major form of academic writing, the research article. We will look at the role that this type of article plays in the typical academic career and then offer some general advice about the organization and length of the research article. In later chapters we'll look in more detail at ways to develop and organize parts of such articles.

The Role of the Research Article

As we have indicated in previous chapters, there is generally an inverse relationship between how much time and effort it takes to write something and how prestigious or valuable it is for the writer. Thus, reviews and conference papers carry less weight than response articles, which in turn carry less weight than research articles. A research article is more difficult to produce because you have to synthesize and respond to the entire literature on a subject (instead of, say, to a single article, as when writing a response).

Because research articles require extra time and planning, it's not unusual to find academics whose vitas boast numerous reviews and conference papers, but few genuine research articles. While this imbalance is understandable in academics early in their careers, it can be fatal at a later stage.

Chapter 7: The Research Article

In our experience, the fewer research articles someone has published, the more difficult he or she will find advancement. It's possible to get hired into an instructor or assistant professor position without research articles, but it's increasingly difficult to advance beyond entry level (i.e., into a tenured associate professorship) without them. And it's next to impossible today to be promoted to full professor without a substantial number of such articles (or books). The lesson is clear: the earlier that you start publishing research articles, the greater your chance of attaining better positions later in your career.

You should also be aware of two situations to approach with caution when planning a research article. One is contributing an article to a collection of essays being edited by someone else. This situation appears attractive, at first glance, because you circumvent the process of figuring out which journal to send your article to, the possibility of having an article rejected by several journals, and so forth. Instead, you are responding to a call for essays, with an announced subject matter, issued by the editor of the collection (similar to a call for papers for a conference). In fact, it may be fairly easy to get your proposal or article accepted by the editor of the collection. The problem is that the editor typically does not have a publisher for the volume *before* the collection is put together. Thus, you may submit an article and have it tied up for months (or longer) while the editor puts together the rest of the submissions, only to finally learn that he or she has been unable to find a publisher. (For example, in 1984 we submitted a paper to a collection which did not see print until 1993.) At that point, your article may be too out of date to submit elsewhere. And, if the editor is able to find a publisher for the collection, be prepared to make additional changes to meet the publisher's wishes. In short, contributing an essay to a collection is rarely as straightforward as it may at first seem.

The other situation you should approach with caution is co-authorship. This process, which is much more common in the sciences than in the humanities, does have certain advantages. As the saying goes, "two (or more) heads are better than one." Working with another author can augment your insights into a subject and increase your ability to collect data. Co-authorship can also increase the number of articles you can produce. On the negative side, co-authored pieces (especially where you are not the first author) may be viewed as less prestigious than sole-authored pieces, depending on your field. More seriously, co-authorship necessarily involves sacrificing some control and making some compromises. We'd advise against embarking upon a collaborative effort unless you are comfortable with your co-author's work habits and the quality of his or her thinking and writing. In addition, both authors should establish a clear timetable and division of labor at the beginning of the project. Approached properly, co-authorship can be enjoyable and productive. With the wrong person, though, it can be a frustrating waste of time.

With these points in mind, let's turn to some strategies for organizing and balancing different parts of the research article.

Organization

Publishable research papers fall into two types: reports of experiments (generally associated with the natural and social sciences) and so-called "desk top research" (generally

Chapter 7: The Research Article

associated with the humanities). Both types have the same three-part structure of PROBLEM-APPROACH-SOLUTION, although the headings that identify each of these sections might go under different names in any given paper. (This is one reason that the structure of a particular paper may not always be transparent.)

Problem. All papers have a PROBLEM section, where the rationale for writing the paper is laid out. That is, there is some unsolved problem or unanswered question in the literature, or there is an inconsistency in the literature, or there is some unexplained phenomenon, and so on. The following passages from various articles all articulate some sort of problem that the author is trying to solve.

Example 1

> Many of those who contribute [to the research on discourse] disagree about how to identify various parts of clauses, about what to call them, and about what roles they play. (Vande Kopple 1991: 311)

In this article, the reader expects (and gets) a metric for identifying parts of clauses and an account of how they affect the flow of information in discourse.

Example 2

> Recent articles about technical writing tend to criticize the traditional objectivity criterion which would contrast technical writing with the subjectivity of literature in general. . . . but such discussions have failed to account for the general feeling that technical writing is distinctively associated with objective reality. (Manning 1988: 241)

Chapter 7: The Research Article

In this article, the reader expects (and gets) a theory of the distinction between literary and technical discourse which explains the perception that technical writing is more "objective" than literary writing.

Example 3

> Textbooks generally advise writers to include an explanation in so-called "negative messages" (traditionally as part of the "indirect plan"). Textbook authors advise that letters containing bad news should be logical and courteous, and they include example letters which are designed to illustrate these qualities. Unfortunately, as Hagge (1989, p. 50) has recently observed about textbook discussions of politeness, "What these textbooks ignore is the real issue: how courtesy is *linguistically encoded* in texts." *(Campbell 1990: 357)*

In this article, the reader expects (and gets) an explanation of how politeness is a function of specific linguistic features of a text.

Examples like these are easy to find. Every worthwhile research paper contains some statement within the first page or two of some problem in search of a solution. Without this section the reader does not understand the author's reason for writing the paper; the reader is left asking, "Why is it important for me to know this?"

Approach. All research papers have an APPROACH section, where the technical, theoretical, or background information necessary to solve the problem is explained to the reader. That is, there is always some key information that the reader needs in order to follow the solution laid out in the paper. For example, in his article entitled "Themes, Thematic

Progressions, and Some Implications for Understanding Discourse," Vande Kopple (1991) uses his approach section to define theme and rheme, as well as different types of themes (ideational, interpersonal, and textual) and to show the reader how to identify each of them. The author introduces his approach section as follows.

> To understand Halliday's division of a clause into one or more themes and a rheme, one must have some knowledge of the three kinds of meaning that Halliday says language conveys: the ideational, the interpersonal, and the textual. In the cases of many clauses, all three kinds of meaning are manifest. (Vande Kopple 1991: 318)

Without this section the reader will not understand the author's solution to the problem; the reader is left asking, "Why is this so confusing?"

Solution. All papers have a SOLUTION section, where the author's approach is applied to some domain of data in order to solve the problem set out in the first section of the paper. That is, there is always some sort of closure. This doesn't mean that the author solves the problem once and for all time, but rather that the author at least proposes a workable (but not indisputable) solution to the problem. In Vande Kopple's paper the solution section applies the theme/rheme approach to actual pieces of writing to illustrate how problems in tone, style, and organization can be solved. The author introduces his solution section as follows.

> Halliday's analysis of clauses into one or more themes and a rheme may lead writing researchers to insights into at least the

following seven aspects of discourse production, structure, or reception. (Vande Kopple 1991: 327)

Without this section the reader feels that his or her time has been wasted; the reader is left asking, "What's the author's point?"

This PROBLEM-APPROACH-SOLUTION organization may not be obvious at first glance since most writers do not use these terms as headings. Consider, for example, Vande Kopple's headings (and our translation of them). (Parentheses indicate that the section is not actually labeled.)

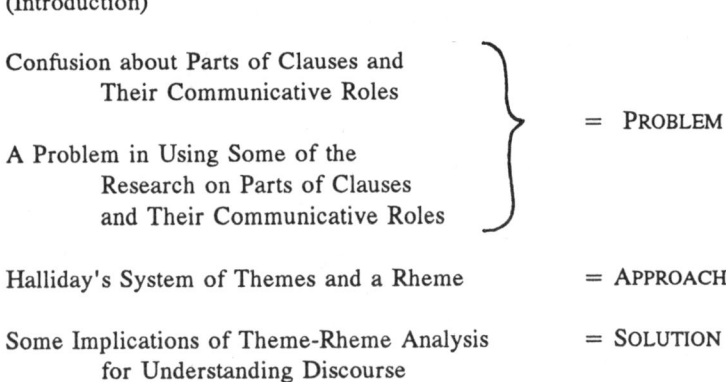

(Introduction)

Confusion about Parts of Clauses and
    Their Communicative Roles

A Problem in Using Some of the
    Research on Parts of Clauses
    and Their Communicative Roles

} = PROBLEM

Halliday's System of Themes and a Rheme   = APPROACH

Some Implications of Theme-Rheme Analysis   = SOLUTION
    for Understanding Discourse

Vande Kopple spells out his PROBLEM over three sections. The unlabelled introduction points out the general problems of terminological confusion and applying existing research. Then he takes each of these up separately in the next two sections; note that the words *Confusion* and *Problem* cue the reader to the nature of these sections. Also, note that the use of jargon terms (*Themes* and *Rheme*) in the next heading help identify it as the APPROACH section, and the use of the term *Implications* in the last heading marks it as the SOLUTION section.

The PROBLEM-APPROACH-SOLUTION headings can be even more transparent. For example, in "*You*-perspective: Insights from Speech Act Theory," Campbell et al. (1990) report the results of desk-top research. The headings they use are given below.

(Introduction)

Current Treatments of the *You*-Perspective = PROBLEM

Linguistic Concepts
    Speech Acts
    Semantic Roles = APPROACH
    Interaction of Speech Act Categories
      and Semantic Roles

Relevance of Speech Act Theory to *You*-Perspective = SOLUTION

Conclusion

These headings are essentially formulaic: *Current Treatments* (of X) = PROBLEM; *Linguistic Concepts* (including Y) = APPROACH; and *Relevance of* (Y to X) = SOLUTION.

In contrast to the headings used in "desk top" research, the following correspondence is typical of that found in experimental papers.

Review of Literature   = PROBLEM
Methodology   = APPROACH
Discussion   = SOLUTION

For example, in "Passive Voice and Rhetorical Role in Scientific Writing," Riley (1991) reports the results of an experimental investigation. The headings she uses are given below.

(Introduction)   = PROBLEM

Description of this Study   = APPROACH

Results   ⎫
                                 ⎬   = SOLUTION
Discussion: Rhetorical Implications ⎭

Conclusion

Note, incidentally, that the heading *Results* generally indicates the raw data generated by an experiment, whereas the heading *Discussion* (or *Findings*) indicates the interpretation of those data.

Length

Besides having headings that underscore the PROBLEM-APPROACH-SOLUTION structure of your paper, it's also important to have the right *balance* among the three sections. You have to assume that your reader is primarily interested in the solution to your problem. That is, the reader needs a clear

Chapter 7: The Research Article

statement of the problem and the approach you will take, but what he or she really wants is a detailed account of your solution. Thus, your reader expects the greatest number of pages of your paper to be devoted to the solution.

Vande Kopple (1991) devotes the following number of pages to the major sections of his paper.

    PROBLEM   =   7 pages
    APPROACH   =   8 pages
    SOLUTION   =   17 pages

This allocation of space to each of the three sections shows the proper emphasis on the SOLUTION. Note that the PROBLEM and APPROACH sections are about equally balanced and that the SOLUTION section takes up more than half of the paper.

Likewise, in "Tone as a Function of Presupposition in Technical and Business Writing," Riley and Parker (1988) devote more than half of their space to the SOLUTION section, as follows.

(Introduction)

Treatments of Tone by
    Writing Specialists   = PROBLEM   = 2 pages

An Alternative Treatment of Tone   = APPROACH   = 3 pages

Presupposition Triggers   = SOLUTION   = 9 pages

Conclusion

On the other hand, problems arise when these sections are not properly balanced. For example, in "The Given/New Contract and Cohesion: Some Suggestions for Classroom Practice," Thompson (1985) attempts to take a specific domain of linguistic theory and show how it can be used in the classroom to effect change in student behavior. Note, however, that she devotes less than one-third of her space to the SOLUTION section, as follows.

(Introduction)	= PROBLEM	= ½ page
The Given/New Contract } Cohesion }	= APPROACH	= 4 pages
Classroom Applications	= SOLUTION	= 2 pages

Simple inspection of the relative space allocated to each of her sections shows that Thompson's paper will probably be of limited use to its audience (i.e., technical writing teachers). The PROBLEM is defined too briefly (in only one-half page), and the APPROACH section is twice as long as the SOLUTION.

Likewise, in "Linguistics, Technical Writing, and Generalized Phrase Structure Grammar," Harris (1988) tries to show that a particular brand of grammar (generalized phrase structure grammar) has pedagogical advantages over others (in particular, transformational grammar). Note, however, that Harris allocates less than 15 percent of his space to the SOLUTION section, as follows.

Chapter 7: The Research Article

```
(Introduction)                        = PROBLEM    = 1 page

The Wax and Wane of        ⎫
  Transformational Grammar ⎬
                           ⎬ = APPROACH  = 8 pages
Generalized Phrase Structure ⎬
  Grammar                  ⎭

Applications to Technical Writing  = SOLUTION  = 2 pages
```

Harris' paper suffers from the same imbalance as Thompson's: a hastily defined PROBLEM (one page) and an APPROACH section that's *four times* the length of the SOLUTION.

In sum, all publishable research papers have a section on each of the following: PROBLEM, APPROACH, and SOLUTION; and the headings the author uses should reflect the content of each of these sections in a reasonably transparent fashion. Moreover, the SOLUTION section of the paper is generally at least twice as long as the PROBLEM and APPROACH sections combined.

Chapter 8: Introductions

The most important function of the introduction is to serve as a "map" to guide the reader through the rest of the paper. At the same time, the introduction must engage the reader *quickly* and *convincingly*. Most readers, contrary to what you might think, are looking for a reason *not* to read your work. At the first sign that you might waste their time, readers will happily dismiss your paper and turn to someone else's. This means you must include just enough information to convince readers that you know what you're talking about, but that you will not abuse their patience.

At minimum, the introduction to a research article has to establish four points for the reader: the subject matter of the paper; the writer's thesis or angle on the subject matter; the relation of the article to previous work--what we might call the writer's entry point into the subject; and the writer's plan for presenting the rest of the article. Consider, for example, the short introduction to Riley's paper, "Conversational Implicature and Unstated Meaning in Professional Communication." (The sentences have been numbered for ease of reference.)

ENTRY POINT	(1) Specialists in technical and business communication have recently called for additional research into the validity of traditionally accepted rhetorical strategies (see, for example, Ewing 1983, Gieselman 1983, Haselkorn 1984, and
TOPIC	Moran and Moran 1985). (2) Toward this end, this article discusses how the theory of conversational

Chapter 8: Introductions

THESIS

implicature, as developed by Grice (1975) and other linguists working within pragmatics, provides insight into he way that readers interpret implied messages. (3) An understanding of how readers infer unstated meaning can be useful in evaluating commonly recommended strategies for negative messages, especially the use of an implied, rather than an explicit, presentation of the negative message.

PROBLEM

(4) The first section of this article reviews the properties that distinguish a negative letter from a positive or persuasive one and summarizes the advice commonly offered for conveying negative messages. (5) The second section outlines the main tenets of Grice's theory of conversational implicature, and also briefly discusses sociolinguistic explanations for the use of indirectness in negative messages. (6) The final section analyzes the texts of several letters, showing how the reader's interpretation of implied messages is explained by Grice's theory. (1988b: 94)

APPROACH

SOLUTION

Note that this introduction consists of two paragraphs containing three sentences each. The first paragraph serves as a "map" of the author's idea, and the second paragraph serves as a "map" of the author's presentation.

Note, moreover, that each sentence serves a specific function. In the idea section, sentence (1) establishes the author's ENTRY POINT for investigating this topic, by invoking other researchers who have called for more work on rhetorical strategies. (This part of the introduction often contains some review of the literature: a survey of what has, or has not, been done on a subject.) Note that this is a more persuasive technique than if the author had merely stated that *she* thought such research was needed. Sentence (2) establishes the author's TOPIC, that is, the subject matter of her paper. She states that she will explain how Grice's theory of implicature accounts for the way readers infer implied meaning. Sentence (3) establishes the author's THESIS; that is, the actual claim she will attempt to support in her paper. She states that she will use the theory of implicature to explain textbook strategies for delivering bad news. Note the difference between a topic (the subject) and a thesis (the claim). The author's topic is implicature; her thesis is that implicature provides a principled explanation for textbook advice.

The distinction between a topic and a thesis is important to understand, because all research papers have a topic but only the publishable ones have both a topic and a thesis. A topic is simply a subject area. For example, managerial communication is a topic. A topic may be wide (e.g., differences between oral and written communication among managers) or narrow (e.g., the sentence structure used in performance appraisals written by managers in a particular company). A thesis, on the other hand, is a claim about a topic. For example, "managerial communication differs from other types of nonacademic communication" is a thesis; "business-writing textbooks present an inaccurate view of managerial communication" is a thesis; and so on.

In the section of the introduction that maps out the author's presentation, sentence (4) describes the PROBLEM section of her paper, where she will define "negative letters" and discuss commonplace textbook advice for constructing them. Sentence (5) describes the APPROACH section of her paper, where she will define implicature and explain how it operates. Sentence (6) describes the SOLUTION section of her paper, where she will analyze several bad news letters, showing how they adhere to Grice's theory of implicature.

Besides extending past research, another way of getting into a paper is to note a GAP in the literature. The following excerpts from the introduction to the article "Managers as Writers" by Smeltzer and Thomas illustrate this approach.

GAP   Most attention in the management literature . . . is either given to oral communication or to communication in general, without distinguishing between oral and written communication. For example, in the past decade not one article in the *Academy of Management Journal* was committed to written managerial communication, whereas several addressed some aspect of oral communication; others addressed communication but did not differentiate between written and oral communication (Schweiger and DeNise; Marcus and Goodman).

Written communication takes place in a different context than oral communication (Daft, Lengel, and Trevino), requires different processing (Liggett), and has different outcomes (Feldman and March). Written communication, however, would seem to be quite important to the management process. Bazerman and Paradis contend that writing structures our relations with others; such structuring is an essential managerial process. But what do we know about managers as written communicators within organizations? (1994: 186-187)

In this example, the authors cite a series of studies to show that they have "done their homework" and that they have discovered what they think is a significant gap in the existing research. This gap, in turn, provides their ENTRY POINT into the subject.

Chapter 8: Introductions

A third common method for getting into a paper is to notice a CONTRADICTION in the literature and make an attempt to reconcile opposing points of view. For example, Riley uses this strategy in her introduction to "Passive Voice and Rhetorical Role in Scientific Writing."' Since the introduction to this paper is fairly long (three pages), we will omit some of the detail here.

> CONTRADICTION Textbooks have typically warned writers to avoid the passive voice [cites examples from the literature]. If, however, we look at actual scientific texts (rather than advice about how these texts should be written), we find that the passive voice is a common feature of such discourse [cites supporting studies]. As a way of reconciling these conflicting viewpoints, some analysts have advised writers to use the passive voice when it is "appropriate" or "necessary" [cites examples from the literature]. [H]owever, this modified approach raises new questions and problems: namely, exactly how can a writer determine when the passive voice is "appropriate" or "necessary"? [Lists other problems.] [W]e need additional analyses of the systems and principles that lead writers to choose passive voice in some rhetorical situations but not in others [cites related studies]. (1991: 239-241)

The author doesn't get to her actual thesis until the first two sentences of the section following the introduction, labelled "Description of This Study." Here she states:

> THESIS The study which follows continues to investigate the relation between the rhetorical roles assumed by scientific writers and the syntactic structures that reflect and reinforce these roles. More specifically, this study addresses the question of whether changes in rhetorical role within a particular

Chapter 8: Introductions

> scientific text are paralleled by changes in the relative number of passive and active structures." (1991: 241)

The logic of her introduction is as follows:

- Textbook advice regarding passive voice is contradicted by actual scientific writing.
- This contradiction has led to a compromise position: use passive voice when "appropriate."
- The compromise position raises unanswered questions.
- These questions can be addressed only through additional studies.
- The current study will attempt to correlate active and passive voice with specific rhetorical roles.

Note, incidentally, the way the author makes the transition in her introduction to the second section of her paper, a description of her study. The very first sentence of the second section is transitional; she states, "The study which follows *continues* to investigate . . . ." The word *continue* establishes the connection between past research and her paper.

In short, the introduction essentially answers four questions: (1) What's the problem? (2) What's been said about it by others? (3) What have I got to say about it? and (4) How am I going to say it?

Chapter 9: Examples

Every publishable piece of writing is crucially dependent upon examples. The most important function of examples is to serve as "bridges" between the abstract (i.e., the unfamiliar) and the concrete (i.e., the familiar). Additionally, examples provide evidence to support the thesis established in your introduction. Consider an article by Flower et al. entitled "Detection, Diagnosis, and the Strategies of Revision." They use the following example to explain the difference between merely *detecting* an error in a piece of writing and *diagnosing* the problem:

> For instance, if a friend looked at us and said, "You're looking peaked today; you'd better get some rest," we would be pleased they cared and even *detected* our terminal condition. If, however, our doctor said that after we had dragged our sorry case to his office, we would no doubt be annoyed, since from him we expect a well-defined, informed diagnosis that provides specific information about the problem and a suggestion for what to do (e.g., "You have infectious mononucleosis with a white blood count of 12,000. I want you to plan on no alcohol and sleeping 10 hours a night for the next two weeks"). A *diagnosis*, in this setting, is a problem representation you would be willing to pay for. (1986: 41; italics added)

This example is quite memorable and works well here because the point the authors are trying to explain is neither technical nor terribly abstract.

Chapter 9: Examples

Most academic writing, however, is either technical or abstract (or both). In such cases, examples have to be carefully constructed in three parts: an abstraction, an illustration, and an interpretation. The ABSTRACTION is a simple statement of the point you're trying to get the reader to understand. The ILLUSTRATION consists of actual data that supports the abstraction. The INTERPRETATION is a statement which spells out for the reader exactly how the illustration embodies the abstraction.

In "Grammar and Technical Writing," Ferguson and Parker use the following example to explain the concept of thematic progression to an audience of technical writing professionals.

ABSTRACTION   The given and new information within each sentence also make up larger patterns over a discourse. This larger organization is called thematic progression. For instance, a linear thematic progression might be represented as A-B, B-C, where the new information (B) in one sentence becomes the old information (B) in the next, as in (11a) and (11b).

ILLUSTRATION
11a.   Epic poems usually include *a long narrative or story*.
11b.   *This story* is almost always marked by certain conventions.

INTERPRETATION   The new information in (11a) includes *story*, which becomes the given information in (11b), *this story*. (1990: 364)

This example illustrates the three-part structure of a complete example:

Chapter 9: Examples

- The first paragraph constitutes the ABSTRACTION. These three sentences simply define thematic progression and, in particular, linear thematic progression. Without this part of the example, the reader would be forced to *infer* the principle being illustrated.

- Sentences (11a-b) constitute the ILLUSTRATION. Without this part of the example, the reader would be forced to *infer* how the principle might apply to specific sentences. (Note that parts of these sentences were italicized in the original text to focus the reader's attention on specific words.)

- The last sentence is the INTERPRETATION. Its only function is to ensure that the reader understands how the illustration embodies the abstraction. Without this part of the example the reader would be forced to *infer* the connection between the principle and the illustration, that is, that *story* is new information in (11a) but given information in (11b).

When we think of using examples in a paper, we tend to think of technical examples, like the one just discussed. Let's now consider how our structure of ABSTRACTION-ILLUSTRATION-INTERPRETATION applies in less technical cases. In "Pragmatics and Technical Communication: Some Further Considerations," Riley uses the following example to counter Haselkorn's claim that pragmatics is a unified field. (Sentences have been numbered for ease of reference.)

Chapter 9: Examples

ABSTRACTION

(1) One problem with Haselkorn's discussion is that he writes as if there were a consensus within current linguistic theory about how to define pragmatics. (2) In fact, however, the field of pragmatics has been, and continues to be, influenced by a number of diverse traditions. (3) For example, Dillon et al. (1985) hold that there are at least "three broad schools or approaches to the study of use," which they label as "the Philosophers, the Data Gatherers, and the Close Readers" (446). (4) And they note that "The past decade can be characterized as a time of excited searching for the right conceptual tools and methods to investigate the relation of utterances to contexts and situations, to actions and events, to participants and their relationships" (446).

ILLUSTRATION

INTERPRETATION

(5) Both Gazdar (1979) and Levinson (1983), in surveying past and present definitions of pragmatics, cite an even greater number of approaches--for example, those of Morris (1938), Carnap (1938), Bar-Hillel (1954), Kalish (1967), Montague (1968), and Katz (1977). (6) In addition, Levinson himself formulates at least four tentative definitions of pragmatics--each of which, he is quick to point out, has its advantages and limitations. (7) The crucial point to note is the diversity of past and present approaches to pragmatics, none of which Haselkorn either acknowledges or aligns himself with. (1986: 161)

Sentences (1-2) constitute the ABSTRACTION: Riley's claim that, contrary to Haselkorn's implication, pragmatics is a diverse field. Sentences (3-6) constitute the ILLUSTRATION. Here, however, the illustration is simply a series of studies and quotations from studies which support her claim in the abstraction. Sentence (7) constitutes the INTERPRETATION, where Riley reminds the reader of the relevance of her

Chapter 9: Examples

illustration to the abstraction, namely, that her data show that Haselkorn's claim is incorrect.

Problems in the use of examples arise when one or more of the three essential parts are omitted. Compare the three-part examples we have looked at so far to one that consists entirely of ABSTRACTION, without any illustration or interpretation. In "Writing Reader-Based Instructions: Strategies to Build Coherence," Mulcahy attempts to define for the reader van Dijk and Kintsch's concept of coherence, as follows. (Sentences have been numbered for ease of reference.)

> (1) Whereas the text paradigm provides a scaffolding for events in the task and cohesive ties provide markers for those events, the macrostructure of the text provides a common theme and a common goal for the task. (2) The van Dijk and Kintsch (1983) processing model of discourse defines a macrostructure as a network of propositions or idea units that the reader creates when reading a text. (3) When processing a text, the reader relates new ideas with ideas active in memory and makes connections among ideas, forming a network of propositions. (4) Coherence in the van Dijk and Kintsch model depends on the number of shared references among idea units . . . . (1988: 236)

This type of pure abstraction conveys little useful information to the reader. This is supposed to be an explication of coherence, but it is phrased entirely of technical terms without any illustration or interpretation. For example, in sentence (1), what is a "text paradigm"? In sentence (2), what are "idea units"? In sentence (3), what is a "network of propositions"? In sentence (4), what is a "shared reference"? These are all terms that are left undefined by Mulcahy, rendering her discussion less than fully informative. Even though this

Chapter 9: Examples

passage "sounds" very learned, its deficiencies become clear when you try to *use* the information in it to judge the coherence of a particular piece of writing.

In contrast, consider Campbell's explication of the closely related concept of cohesion, which she defines as "the result of repeating semantic and structural elements" (1991: 222). She states:

ABSTRACTION 1

ILLUSTRATION 1

In his article establishing the relevance of perceptual phenomena to the study of discourse, Manning writes that "a clear perception of differences demands a common background of similarity against which differences may stand out" [14, p. 244]. To illustrate, find the "O" in each of the figures in Figure 1.

REPETITION AND COHESION

	(1)		(2)	
		XTKLPWXE		XXXXXXXX
		HWIZKLSQ		XXXXXXXX
		PWEJVODF		XXXXXOXX
		RHCTUGBN		XXXXXXXX

Figure 1. This figure demonstrates the role of repetition in perceptions of cohesion.

INTERPRETATION 1

ABSTRACTION 2

Although each "O" appears in the same row and column of each figure, it is significantly easier to locate the "O" in (2) because the repetition of X's provides a uniform background against which the "O" is distinctive. In an early study of cohesion, Bellert noted that part of "the coherence of a text consists, roughly speaking, in repetitions [15, p. 336]. I want to suggest that textual cohesion (both written and oral) is analogous to the perceptual phenomenon illustrated by the X's in (2).

ILLUSTRATION 2

Consider the example below [16, p. 36].

Chapter 9: Examples

INTERPRETATION 2

<u>The aim of the</u> Platonic <u>philosophy was to</u> exalt <u>man</u> into God. <u>The aim of the</u> Baconian <u>was to</u> provide <u>him</u> with what he required while he continues to be a man.

Note that the underlined portions of these two sentences are repetitive. In other words, the syntactic pattern of these sentences is parallel. In my view, both writers and readers use the repetition of elements such as the sentence pattern above as a background of similarity against which differences in meaning can be more easily produced and perceived. (1991: 224-225)

In this passage, Campbell essentially gives two examples, one from the visual realm and one from the textual. Each example, in turn, consists of ABSTRACTION-ILLUSTRATION-INTERPRETATION.

We should also note that simply using a three-part structure does not guarantee an effective example. For instance, In "Linguistics, Technical Writing, and Generalized Phrase Structure Grammar," Harris uses the following example for an audience composed primarily of technical writing professionals. The example is intended to explain the relationship of active to passive voice.

In Phrase Structure terms, Chomsky noticed that the Immediate Constituent model entailed a vast number of unproductive redundancies, of the type illustrated in 1.

1. a. $S \longrightarrow NP+V+NP$
   b. $S \longrightarrow NP+be+V+by+NP$

That is, he noticed a Phrase Structure account of language, on its own, required two independent rules to generate (or describe, or predict) the sentences of 2.

Chapter 9: Examples

ILLUSTRATION   2.   a.   Rambo killed the commies.
                                   b.   The commies were killed by Rambo.

ABSTRACTION   Two essential facts about passives are consequently unavailable to a grammar which uses the independent rules of 1 to generate the sentences of 2. First, 2a and 2b, like virtually all active-passive pairs, mean the same thing (at least propositionally). Second, there is a very systematic formal relationship between them, shared by all active-passive pairs: the order of the NPs is always inverse; the second NP in the passive always pairs with *by*; and the auxiliary verb *be* precedes the passive main verb, which must be a past participle. All of this looks entirely accidental in the description 1 offers; two rules, two structures, end of account. (1988: 229)

This example is divided into three parts; however, they do not match the ABSTRACTION-ILLUSTRATION-INTERPRETATION paradigm we have set up. The text down to (2a-b) contains abstract terms, but does not constitute an abstraction. It makes no general claim about the topic of the passage (i.e., the passive/active relationship), and the formalism it contains is gratuitous. Sentences (2a-b) constitute the ILLUSTRATION, and everything following the illustration is the ABSTRACTION. Note, however, that the INTERPRETATION section is missing completely and that the other two are reversed.

The most significant problem in this example is that the reader is presented with the illustration before he or she has any idea of what it is supposed to exemplify. This is evidenced by the fact that topic of the example (i.e., passives) is not even mentioned until the first line *following* the illustration: "Two essential facts about passives are . . . ." For these reasons, it would be difficult, if not impossible, for

Chapter 9: Examples

linguistically naive readers (like those for whom Harris is writing) to get much at all out of this example.

Before leaving the subject of examples, it is worth discussing the difference between CONSTRUCTED and LIVE illustrations. Consider the following explication of the concept of implicature, by Parker and Campbell.

ABSTRACTION	An implicature, as defined by Grice in "Logic and Conversation," is information that is reasonably inferred from an utterance but does not follow
CONSTRUCTED ILLUSTRATION	necessarily from that utterance. For example, if a speaker were to say "Mrs. Jones has two daughters," then it is *necessarily true* that Mrs. Jones has one daughter. On the other hand, one can *reasonably infer* from this utterance that Mrs. Jones has no more than two daughters, even though this does not follow necessarily. That is, the proposition `Mrs. Jones has two daughters' is true even if she has three daughters.
LIVE ILLUSTRATION	Walzer applies the concept of "reasonable inference" to the creation of false implicatures in professional writing. He gives the example of a writer preparing a proposal for a potential buyer of a health insurance policy. He is counting on his company's "guaranteed renewable clause" to lead the reader to infer that the company will renew policies as long as the premiums are paid, even though he knows the clause, in insurance jargon, only commits the company to renew policies until the holder reaches age 50 or for 5 years. What the writer says is not technically false, but the implicature it raises is. (1993: 308-309)

The first illustration (the one about Mrs. Jones' daughters) was constructed by Parker and Campbell essentially to "teach" the

Chapter 9: Examples

reader the concept of implicature very briefly. Note, incidentally, that the essence of implicature (reasonable inference) is conveyed by contrasting it to another concept (necessary truth). On the other hand, the second illustration (the one about the insurance policy) is an actual instance of implicature in operation. This illustration was selected to show how implicature affects our perceptions in everyday life. The most important point to note here is that both the constructed and the live illustration have necessary though different functions. The insurance example would not be very effective in trying to explain the essence of implicature to a naive reader, and the daughter example would surely fail to show the reader how implicature affects our perceptions in everyday situations.

The use of illustrations in examples is the mark of a writer who understands the concepts under discussion. A piece of writing without illustrations is a clear indication that the writer doesn't understand the material. Problems can also arise, however, when a writer relies entirely on illustrations from another source. For example, Lovejoy, in an article entitled "The Gricean Model: A Revising Rubric," borrows directly from Paul Grice:

ABSTRACTION . . . Grice uses this example to show how the maxim of Quantity may be flouted in a writing situation:

ILLUSTRATION A is asked to write a testimonial about a pupil who is a candidate for a philosophy job, and his letter reads as follows: "Dear Sir, Mr. X's command of English is excellent, and his attendance at tutorials has been regular. Yours, etc."

INTERPRETATION A cannot be unwilling to cooperate because if A were, A would not be writing in the first place. A knows that more

Chapter 9: Examples

> information than this is expected, and A is capable of furnishing this information because X is his student. It follows then that A is implicating what he is reluctant to express in words--that Mr. X is not a good candidate for the philosophy job. (1987: 10-11)

Note that even though this example consists of an ABSTRACTION, ILLUSTRATION, and INTERPRETATION, they are all from Grice's original work--either direct quotes or paraphrases. This suggests that Lovejoy is apparently unable to illustrate Grice's ideas with his *own* illustrations; the reader can only infer that Lovejoy doesn't understand the concepts well enough to illustrate them. To make matters worse, this is the *only* example Lovejoy gives in a nine-page article!

In short, the essence of academic writing is didactic: to explain theories to the reader. Effective explanations, in turn, are always couched in terms of examples, which form a "bridge" from the familiar (the concrete) to the remote (the abstract). Think about it: the understanding you get from reading an article, you get from the *examples*. To be effective, an example must consist of three facets: an abstraction, an illustration, and an interpretation.

Chapter 10: Quotations

Quotations cannot be surpassed for adding authority to an argument. For example, consider the following passage, where a quotation is used to give authority to a point the writers are trying to make.

> The distinctions among theory, application, and practice are summarized in Table 1. This three-way distinction, in turn, is implicit in the organization of academic fields. Kuhn, for example, notes that "The process of learning a *theory* depends upon the study of *applications*, including *practice* problem-solving both with a pencil and paper and with instruments in the laboratory" (47; emphasis added) (Parker & Campbell, 1993: 301)

Here the authors use a quotation from Kuhn, a well-known and respected philosopher of science, to augment their distinction among theory, application, and practice. In other words, it's not just the authors who make this distinction, but famous thinkers as well. Note, too, that they have highlighted the relevance of the quote to their point by italicizing the three words of Kuhn that they are focusing on: "theory," "applications," and "practice."

The quote from Kuhn above is easy to use since Kuhn's terminology (i.e., *theory*, *applications*, and *practice*) matches the authors' exactly. Often, however, a useful quotation does not use the terminology of interest, so it has to be "translated" into the writer's terms. Consider, for example, the following

Chapter 10: Quotations

quotation, which is used in the same article to support the distinction among theory, application, and practice:

> . . . two questions . . . have persisted in composition circles. One is "How are we supposed to apply linguistics in composition?" Regarding this question, Crowley states, "Paul Roberts felt that while linguistic science could `provide . . . certain *basic principles* [i.e., theory] and much relevant data,' it could not `as science, say anything' at all about *the uses* [i.e., application] to which these principles and data are to be put or *the methods* [i.e., practice] by which they are to be purveyed . . . . Such a program, presumably, would be developed by teachers, rather than by scholars in linguistics" (500; emphasis added). (Parker & Campbell, 1993: 303)

Note that the quotation from Crowley does not mention the words *theory*, *application*, or *practice*. The authors, however, have identified three synonymous terms in the quote (i.e., "basic principles," "uses," and "methods") and have highlighted them with italics. Then, the authors essentially translated each of these terms into *theory*, *application*, and *practice*, respectively, by adding them within brackets. The point to note is that if the authors had *not* provided this "translation," then the connection between Crowley's quote and the authors' point would have been entirely opaque.

Quotations are especially important in that section of a paper where you criticize someone else's position. Here it is always much more persuasive to use the words of your opponents rather than your own. Consider, for example, the following passage, from "Linguistics and Writing," which criticizes the state of research and teaching in composition:

Chapter 10: Quotations

Compositionists have long been dissatisfied with the quality of theory construction in the field of writing. Crowley, for example, notes the "intellectual poverty that characterized instruction in writing" (481) and ". . . the dreary wasteland that was freshman English at midcentury" (500). She further notes that ". . . a theoretical deficiency had plagued freshman composition for many years . . ." (500). Although the situation has improved in the last 40 years, the status of theory in composition still leaves much to be desired. For example, writing in the early 1980's, Bereiter and Scardamalia bemoan ". . . the miscellaneous character of much writing research . . ." (3). Even more recently, North states that of the various kinds of research in composition, "The result has been an accumulated knowledge of a relatively impressive size, but one that lacks any clear coherence or methodological integrity" (3).

Classroom practice in composition does not fare much better. Milic writes that "Most composition courses proceed under extremely vague notions of the task being attempted and the criteria for improvement. Indeed, it appears probable that many instructors `go through the motions,' . . . and . . . conclude with a grade whose significance is uncertain" (193). Milic adds that part of the reason for the general ineffectiveness of composition instruction is that "Teachers . . . are unable to make a sufficient analysis of the type of error they have noted" (193). The sense of futility felt by composition teachers has been voiced recently by none less than Edward Corbett. He states, "I would have to confess that I do not seem to be doing my students much good. I do not turn my good writers into excellent writers; and I do not detect that my bad writers are any less bad at the end of the term . . . . [A]m I really teaching any of my students how to write? Maybe all of us composition teachers need to ask ourselves that question" (452). Richard Larson did, in fact, ask that question. After a six-year study of 240 colleges, culminating in 1992, he concludes that "first year composition has become simply randomized exposure of students to a writing teacher who may not know a great deal about writing, reading, or teaching" (9). In short, compositionists practicing today are apparently experiencing the same sense of futility and frustration as felt by their colleagues 40 years ago. (Parker & Campbell, 1993: 299-300)

Chapter 10: Quotations

By using quotations from their opponents' writings, the authors achieve two ends they would not achieve with their own words. First, they get to use phraseology they would never get by with otherwise: "intellectual poverty," "dreary wasteland," etc. These kinds of phrases can be used by insiders, people who are a part of the field they are criticizing, but not by outsiders, such as the authors of this work. In other words, the writers get to criticize their subjects without having to take direct responsibility for the criticism itself. Second, the criticism cannot be as easily dismissed since it is being leveled by peers--in fact, well-known and respected peers, not by the outsiders who are the authors of the article. In short, it's always more effective to use people's own words when you're attacking their position.

It's important to understand that quotations, although useful for other purposes, are not adequate substitutes for ILLUSTRATIONS in explicating a concept. Consider Lovejoy's explanation of the Cooperative Principle (paragraphs have been numbered for ease of reference):

> (1) Grice formulates a general principle, called the Cooperative Principle, that speakers in a talk-exchange observe, and he bases it on the assumption that our talk-exchanges are "cooperative efforts" having "a common purpose or set of purposes." The Cooperative Principle (hereafter referred to as the CP) prescribes that what we say in conversation generally coincides with the direction established in the talk-exchange. He defines the CP as follows:
>
> (2) Make your conversational contribution such as is required, at the stage at which it occurs, by the accepted purpose or direction of the talk-exchange in which you are engaged. (1987: 10)

Chapter 10: Quotations

Note the use of quotations from Grice in Lovejoy's first sentence. These are apparently included to give the piece an air of authority. Moreover, this example appears to have the general structure of abstraction (paragraph 1) and illustration (paragraph 2). Upon closer inspection, however, the quote from Grice in (2) is not an illustration of the abstraction in (1) at all, but is itself merely *more* abstraction. Note that a reader of this passage (who was not previously familiar with Grice and his work) would be hard-pressed to give an illustration of the Cooperative Principle in action, based on Lovejoy's discussion.

Mulcahy runs into the same problem in her explication of so-called "causal networks." (Sections have been numbered for ease of reference.)

> (1) According to Trabasso and Sperry (1985), construction of a causal network begins with an opening event. Each succeeding event is then evaluated according to the criterion of "necessity in the circumstances" (Mackie 1980) using counterfactual reasoning (Lewis 1976):
>
>> (2) Event A is said to be necessary for event B in the circumstances in that if A had not occurred, then event B also would not have occurred. A causal relation, by these criteria, defines a logical dependency between A and B. An event is sufficient, in the sense that if event A is put into the circumstances and the events are allowed to go on from there, event B will occur (Trabasso and van den Broek 1985, 617).
>
> (3) A causal chain is constructed to describe the actions towards a goal: if event A causes event B, and event B causes event C, then events A, B and C are joined into a network, A --> B --> C (van den Broek and Trabasso 1986, 3). [1988: 240]

Chapter 10: Quotations

This example also mimics the ABSTRACTION-ILLUSTRATION-INTERPRETATION structure we discussed in Chapter 9. That is, section (1) appears to be an abstraction, (2) an illustration, and (3) an interpretation. Upon closer inspection, however, the entire passage is nothing but abstraction. Note that the three sections could be arranged in *any order* and make just about as much sense. It's indicative also that in section (2), where we expect an illustration, we get nothing but a long abstract quotation from two *other* authors (Trabasso and van den Broek). Then in section (3), where we expect some sort of interpretation of this quote, all we get is more abstraction--this time from *another* article by the same two authors.

In short, the main function of quotations is to lend weight to your argument--either by citing an authority or by arguing against your opponents with their own words. On the other hand, quotations never serve as a substitute for examples.

Chapter 11: Figures

Any writing on a subject that is the least bit complex requires the use of figures. A figure is simply any visual representation of an idea--in essence, a "picture" of an idea. Figures include drawings, pictures, tables, diagrams, charts, and can even include lists. The rule for deciding whether or not to use a figure is straightforward: if it simplifies the concept for the reader (i.e., makes it easier or faster to understand), use it; otherwise don't.

Consider Figure 11.1, taken from "Speech Act Theory and Degrees of Directness in Professional Writing." This half-page figure summarizes two and a half pages of prose discussion, which includes the explication of four principles and nine strategies for creating indirectness. This figure is useful for two reasons. First, it not only summarizes numerous points buried in the prose text, but it also stands out on the page and makes it easier for the reader to go back and refer to from a later point in the article.

Chapter 11: Figures

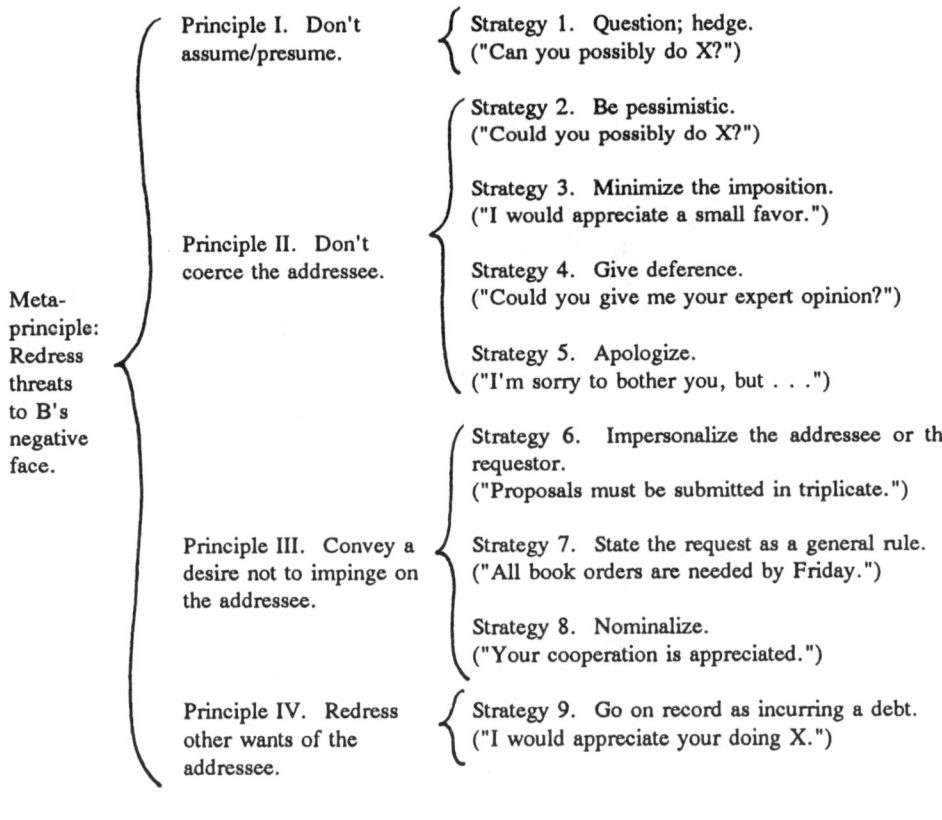

(Riley 1988a:14)

Figure 11.1. Face-Saving Principles and Strategies
with Illustrations

Consider what the same information would have looked like in paragraph format:

> The meta-principle is to redress threats to B's negative face. Principle I is Don't assume/presume. This can be accomplished by

Chapter 11: Figures

> Strategy 1, Question; hedge (e.g., "Can you possibly do X?"). Principle II is Don't coerce B. This can be accomplished by Strategy 2, Be pessimistic (e.g., "Could you possibly do X?"), Strategy 3, Minimize the imposition (e.g., "I would appreciate a small favor"), Strategy 4, Give deference (e.g., "Could you give me your expert opinion?"), or Strategy 5, Apologize (e.g., "I'm sorry to bother you, but . . ."). Principle III is Convey a desire not to impinge on B. This can be accomplished by Strategy 6, Impersonalize the addressee or the requestor (e.g., "Proposals must be submitted in triplicate"), Strategy 7, State the request as a general rule (e.g., "All book orders are needed by Friday"), or Strategy 8, Nominalize (e.g., "Your cooperation is appreciated"). Principle IV is Redress other wants of B's. This can be accomplished by Strategy 9, Go on record as incurring a debt (e.g., "I would appreciate your doing X").

The distinctions among principles, strategies, and illustrations are completely opaque in this format.

Second, Figure 11.1 includes an illustration for each strategy; for example, "Strategy 3. Minimize the imposition. ("I would appreciate a *small* favor.") Without such illustrations, the figure would be almost useless. Consider Figure 11.2, which is identical to 11.1, but without the illustrations. This format is clear, but the content is completely opaque without illustrations.

Before leaving this example, it would be useful to look at some principles for integrating figures into the surrounding prose. In Chapter 9 we looked at the typical three-part structure of the example: ABSTRACTION-ILLUSTRATION-INTERPRETATION. Figures often fill the second of the three roles, serving to illustrate an abstraction. In working a figure into the surrounding text, a good rule of thumb is to use the three "I's": introduce, identify, and interpret the figure. First,

Chapter 11: Figures

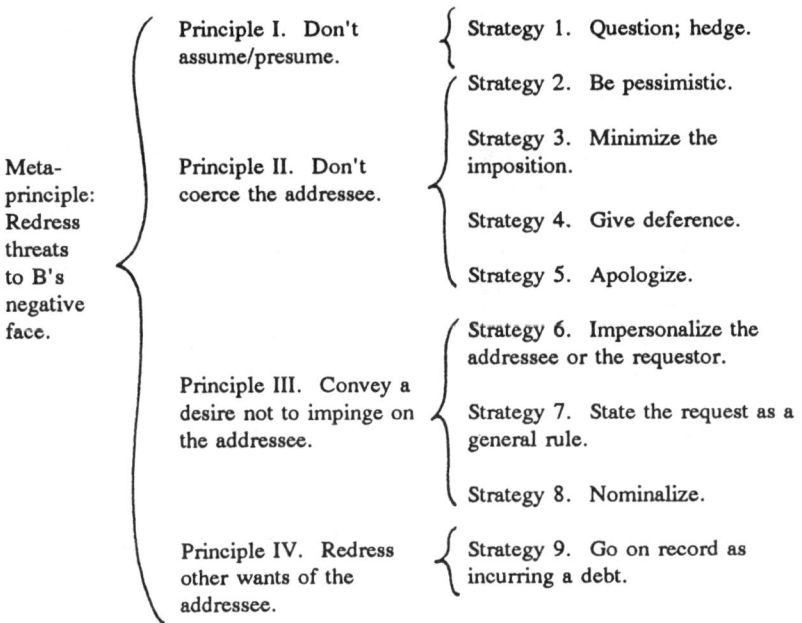

Figure 11.2. Face-Saving Principles and Strategies without Illustrations

introduce the figure by mentioning the abstraction or generalization which it is supposed to illustrate. For example, the following sentence was used to introduce the figure shown on the first page of this chapter, from "Speech Act Theory and Degrees of Directness in Professional Writing":

> Figure [11.1] summarizes the main points of this section so far, and shows the relation between Principles I-IV and Strategies 1-9, along with an example of each strategy in use. (Riley 1988a: 14)

Chapter 11: Figures

Second, identify the figure by giving it a label and number (e.g., "Figure 11.1") and a title or caption (e.g., "Face-Saving Principles and Strategies with Illustrations"). Third, interpret the figure in the text that immediately follows it. The text should draw the reader's attention to the main patterns discernable in the figure--for example, "Note that two of the principles can be achieved by a number of strategies."

The most common error regarding figures is not using one where it is needed. Consider, for example, the following passage from "Cross-Cultural Business Communication Research," which identifies four dimensions of corporate culture.

> Hofstede (1980), investigating the work-related values and attitudes of the employees in several subsidiaries of a large corporation, derived through factor analysis four dimensions of culture that he deemed as salient: Masculinity - Femininity, Individualism - Collectivism, Power Distance, and Uncertainty Avoidance. On the masculinity pole of the masculinity-femininity continuum are values such as productivity, competition, monetary gains and bigness, while on the femininity pole one finds values like quality of life, societal welfare, and cooperation. Individualism is associated with personal time, freedom on the job, challenge, and individual responsibility. Collectivism goes with supportive work environment, goal direction, and group responsibility. High power distance refers to top-down decision making, loyalty to the boss, and rigid hierarchical structure; lower power distance translates into egalitarian work environment, flexible hierarchies, and participative management. High uncertainty avoidance leads to explicit (written) rules and regulations, a great need for long-range planning, and reliance on information systems. Low uncertainty avoidance, on the other hand, means very few formalized rules, low need for MIS, and less preoccupation with long-term planning. (Limaye and Victor, 1991: 290-291)

This paragraph contains some interesting information, but it is difficult for the reader to use (and, for that matter, to find) because it is buried in prose. Consider the difference in effect if it had been presented in a format such as Figure 11.3.

Masculine
productivity
competition
monetary gains

Feminine
quality of life
societal welfare
cooperation

Individualism
personal time/job freedom
challenge
individual responsibility

Collectivism
supportive work environment
goal direction
group responsibility

High Power
top-down decisions
loyalty to boss
rigid hierarchy

Low Power
participative management
egalitarianism
flexible hierarchy

Uncertainty Avoidance
explicit rules
more planning
high MIS need

Uncertainty Acceptance
few rules
less planning
low MIS need

Figure 11.3. Four Dimensions of Corporate Culture

It's worth noting, too, that in constructing this figure from the information provided by Limaye and Victor, we had to *impose* organization not present in their original. For example, the two columns fall naturally into opposites; however, "top-down decision making" is not the opposite of "egalitarian work environment," as Limaye and Victor imply in their prose treatment, but rather of "participative management." On the other hand, we find concepts that don't

Chapter 11: Figures

really seem to make sense. For example, Limaye and Victor imply that the opposite of "challenge" is "goal direction," but it isn't at all clear what "goal direction" means. Moreover, if it means `goal-directed,' then it should probably be a property of "individualism" rather than "collectivism." In short, reducing your prose to figures makes you make sense--not just to the reader but to yourself.

Another source of difficulty is the arrangement of material within a figure. For example, consider the following passage from "A Study of Topic Sentence Use in Technical Writing," which discusses the percentage of topic sentences found in different types of writing. The table in this passage suffers from two problems. First, the organizing principle of the material is, presumably, the percentage of topic sentences in each type of writing. However, note that the rows are not arranged in either ascending or descending order: the right-hand column goes from 54% up to 95%, down to 37%, back up to 55%, and so on. Second, the paragraph preceding the table contrasts the technical writing data with all of the rest (i.e., academic writing, scientific writing, and journalism). However, the table itself does not begin with technical writing but rather with academic writing.

Chapter 11: Figures

Overall topic sentence frequency. As a whole, the writing in the [technical writing] corpus had a low density of topic sentences, with only 32% of all paragraphs containing topic sentences. In fact, it had significantly fewer topic sentences than did academic writing, scientific writing, and popular journalism examined in previous research, as shown in Table 1.

Table 1. Topic Sentence (TS) Frequency in Various Discourse Communities

Discourse Community	Researcher(s)	Corpus Size	TS%
Academic writing (research articles)	Popken (1987)	1477	54%
Academic writing (college textbooks)	Ashton et al. (1985)	829	95%
Popular journalism	Braddock (1974)	889	37%
Scientific writing	Popken (1988)	543	55%
Technical writing	Popken (1989)	700	32%

(Popken, 1991: 51)

The table could be reorganized to better effect as follows, with the technical writing data on top and the rest in ascending order of percentages:

Table 1. Topic Sentence (TS) Frequency in Various Discourse Communities

Discourse Community	Researcher(s)	Corpus Size	TS%
Technical writing	Popken (1989)	700	32%
Popular journalism	Braddock (1974)	889	37%
Academic writing (research articles)	Popken (1987)	1477	54%
Scientific writing	Popken (1988)	543	55%
Academic writing (college textbooks)	Ashton et al. (1985)	829	95%

In the revised version, the reader's attention is focussed on technical writing in contrast to the other forms (since the technical writing data are first), and the reader is given the rank order of discourse forms in terms of their use of topic sentences.

Although a less common problem, occasionally figures are used where they are *not* needed. Consider an example from an article purporting to show the relevance of linguistic theory to technical writing. The article, which was only four pages long, contained three diagrams on three consecutive pages. Moreover, all of Figure 1 was repeated in Figure 2, and all of Figure 2 was repeated in Figure 3. However, if the author had omitted the redundancy, the "article" would have been only two pages long!

In sum, a figure serves as a picture: a visual synopsis of your discussion. Because a figure fits on a single page and, at the same time, summarizes pages of prose, it serves as a reference point for your reader. Stop and think about it--when you go back to an article you have read earlier, but forgotten the main point of, it's the figures that are most helpful in refreshing your memory. A picture really is worth a thousand words. (Maybe more.)

Chapter 12: Metalanguage

METALANGUAGE is phraseology whose main function is to convey authorial commentary on the content of the text itself. Metalanguage, in essence, serves as a series of "guide posts" for your reader. Transitions, for example, are a type of metalanguage. The importance of metalinguistic devices cannot be overestimated. In essence, they tell the reader how to interpret what follows.

Consider, for example, the way Campbell uses metalanguage in her introduction to "Structural Cohesion in Technical Texts." (Sentences have been numbered and phrases underlined for ease of reference.)

(1) In their seminal work, *Cohesion in English*, Halliday and Hasan argue that cohesion is a non-structural, semantic relation. (2) Indeed, cohesion studies of texts using Halliday and Hasan's scheme have proliferated since its publication . . . . (3) Moreover, Witte and Faigley write that "because *Cohesion in English* is a pioneering effort to describe relationships between and among sentences in text, we anticipate that cohesion will be studied in future research addressing the linguistic features of written texts" [p. 199]. (4) In addition, Stotsky notes that Halliday and Hasan's scheme must be modified to accurately represent cohesion in expository essays. (5) Likewise, in her study of cohesion in business writing, Johns writes that the theory "requires further change . . . [because] most of the Halliday and Hasan coding was done on British literature, especially *Alice in Wonderland*; . . . items which appear in Lewis Carroll's writing are not those typical of modern business writing" [p. 41]. (6) Unfortunately, there has been little substantive addition to the theory of cohesion set forth by Halliday and Hasan fifteen years ago, despite its *pioneering* nature.

(7) In this article, I want to suggest that cohesion may be better understood as a general perceptual phenomenon instead of a purely

semantic one. (8) <u>Specifically, I will propose</u> that cohesion is the result of repeating semantic and structural elements. (9) This repetition, <u>in turn</u>, appears to provide a uniform background against which semantic distinctions are foregrounded (much the same as repeated visual patterns form a background against which visual distinctions are foregrounded). (10) <u>Most importantly here, I want to argue</u> that Halliday and Hasan's scheme for coding cohesive devices is descriptively inadequate because of the authors' claim that cohesive relations are semantic, not structural. (11) <u>I believe</u> their exclusion of structural cohesion results partly from their use of a fictional text in formulating their theory. (12) <u>In fact</u>, there appear to be a number of structural cohesive relations in texts. (13) <u>My main purpose</u> here, then, is to substantiate the occurrence of these structural cohesive devices by analyzing a wide variety of technical texts.

(14) <u>To this end, I will first discuss</u> the limitations of Halliday and Hasan's theory of cohesion. (15) <u>Second, I will briefly outline</u> an alternative view of cohesion as a general perceptual phenomenon. (16) <u>And, third, I will present</u> examples of structural cohesion produced through 1) thematic progression, 2) syntactic parallelism, and 3) graphic devices (including the use of typography, enumeration, and charts). (1991: 221-222)

Campbell uses the first paragraph of the introduction to establish the ENTRY POINT into the problem she will attempt to solve. She starts with Halliday and Hasan's claim that cohesion is not a structural property. She then cites ten studies of cohesion based on Halliday and Hasan's theory to show that cohesion is an important concept in the field, of interest to a great many investigators. (She quotes Witte and Faigley to this effect.) She then gives two quotations that establish the need for modifying Halliday and Hasan's theory. She then states her main point in sentence (6): "Unfortunately, there has been little substantive addition to the theory . . . ." Note her use of metalanguage in the first paragraph to lead up to the problem she states in its final sentence: "Indeed" (2), "moreover" (3), "in addition" (4), "likewise" (5) all signal the aggregation of facts and observations; however, "unfortunately" (6) signals

Chapter 12: Metalanguage

that the expectations built up in the first five sentences have not been borne out.

Campbell uses the second paragraph to articulate and explain her THESIS: that cohesion is achieved through the repetition of elements, whether semantic or structural. Once again, she uses metalanguage in achieving this end. In (7), she shifts the reader's attention from other people's work to her own with "In this article . . . ." In (8), she introduces her thesis with "Specifically, I will propose . . . ." In (9), she elaborates on her thesis; this is signaled by the transition "in turn." In (10), she underscores the negative aspect of her thesis (i.e., Halliday and Hasan are wrong) by using "Most importantly here I want to argue . . . ." In (11-12), she elaborates on (10) by using "I believe" and "in fact." In (13) she highlights the positive aspect of her thesis (i.e., cohesion is structural) by using "My main purpose. . . ."

The final paragraph is the "map" of her presentation. Sentence (14) describes the PROBLEM; (15) describes her APPROACH; and (16) describes her SOLUTION. Once again, note Campbell's use of metalanguage: "To this end, I will first discuss . . . ." "Second, I will briefly outline . . . ." "And, third, I will present . . . ."

In all, Campbell's introduction consists of 16 sentences--5 of which contain metalanguage. To appreciate the amount of information conveyed by such devices, we have repeated Campbell's introduction below, *without* the metalanguage.

(1) In their seminal work, *Cohesion in English*, Halliday and Hasan argue that cohesion is a non-structural, semantic relation. (2) Cohesion studies of texts using Halliday and Hasan's scheme have

Chapter 12: Metalanguage

proliferated since its publication . . . . (3) Witte and Faigley write that "because *Cohesion in English* is a pioneering effort to describe relationships between and among sentences in text, we anticipate that cohesion will be studied in future research addressing the linguistic features of written texts" [p. 199]. (4) Stotsky notes that Halliday and Hasan's scheme must be modified to accurately represent cohesion in expository essays. (5) In her study of cohesion in business writing, Johns writes that the theory "requires further change . . . [because] most of the Halliday and Hasan coding was done on British literature, especially *Alice in Wonderland*; . . . items which appear in Lewis Carroll's writing are not those typical of modern business writing" [p. 41]. (6) There has been little substantive addition to the theory of cohesion set forth by Halliday and Hasan fifteen years ago, despite its *pioneering* nature.

(7) Cohesion may be better understood as a general perceptual phenomenon instead of a purely semantic one. (8) Cohesion is the result of repeating semantic and structural elements. (9) This repetition appears to provide a uniform background against which semantic distinctions are foregrounded (much the same as repeated visual patterns form a background against which visual distinctions are foregrounded). (10) Halliday and Hasan's scheme for coding cohesive devices is descriptively inadequate because of the authors' claim that cohesive relations are semantic, not structural. (11) Their exclusion of structural cohesion results partly from their use of a fictional text in formulating their theory. (12) There appear to be a number of structural cohesive relations in texts. (13) The occurrence of these structural cohesive devices can be substantiated by analyzing a wide variety of technical texts.

(14) Halliday and Hasan's theory of cohesion has limitations. (15) There is an alternative view of cohesion as a general perceptual phenomenon. (16) There are examples of structural cohesion produced through 1) thematic progression, 2) syntactic parallelism, and 3) graphic devices (including the use of typography, enumeration, and charts).

In short, metalanguage conveys the author's *attitude* toward the subject; it instructs the reader on how to interpret the text. Without metalanguage the reader learns the "facts" but not their significance.

Chapter 13: Conclusions

For all practical purposes, the conclusion of a paper is essentially a THESIS ABSTRACT of that paper (see Chapter 4). The main difference is that an abstract is a summary typically written *before* you write the paper, and a conclusion is a summary written *after* you write the paper. Both, however, should be self-contained; you don't want to force the reader back into the body of the paper while reading the conclusion.

Consider, for example, the following conclusion from a 19-page article entitled "Tone as a Function of Presupposition in Technical and Business Writing." (Paragraphs have been numbered for ease of reference.)

CONCLUSION

(1) Let us summarize the main points of our discussion. Within the field of professional writing, the problem of tone is usually treated on a case-by-case basis, using what has been termed a "hit-list" approach: "Say this; don't say that." This approach is useful insofar as it provides students, teachers, practitioners, and researchers with specific examples of tone. At the same time, however, a more comprehensive theory of tone (or of any other phenomenon in professional writing) requires an articulation of the general principles that predict and explain particular examples.

(2) We have proposed that the linguistic concept of presupposition (i.e., a proposition implied by a particular linguistic expression) helps to explain how and why a number of problems in tone arise. We have identified two types of presupposition that are relevant to these problems: *existential* presuppositions, which concern

the truth of a proposition, and *evaluative* presuppositions, which concern the writer's attitude toward a proposition. These two types of presuppositions, in turn, account for two different sources of tone problems. One is where the writer and reader disagree about the *truth* of a proposition; the other is where they hold different *value judgments* about a proposition.

(3) By way of illustration, we have discussed several constructions that affect presuppositions directly and tone indirectly.

- A *wh-question* presupposes the truth of the proposition it expresses (e.g., "When may I come in for an interview?" presupposes `I may come in for an interview.'). In contrast, a *conditional* suspends the truth of the proposition it expresses (e.g., "If you want to place an order" allows either the proposition `You want to place an order' or the proposition `You do not want to place an order').
- A *factive predicate* presupposes the truth of the proposition expressed in the complement; a *non-factive predicate* suspends such a proposition (e.g., "You claim that the goods were damaged" suspends the truth of the proposition `The goods were damaged').
- An *implicative predicate* presupposes a proposition expressing a particular attitude (e.g., "You failed to supply your credit card number" presupposes an unmet obligation on the part of the addressee).

(4) We are not arguing that all problems in tone can be explained by presupposition theory in particular or by linguistic theory in general. Rather, we are merely proposing that some problems in tone can be explained by reference to the linguistic concept of presupposition. Nor are we suggesting that courses in professional writing be transformed into linguistic theory classes; such a move would clearly subordinate the ends of instruction to the means. Instead, we are simply arguing that a working knowledge of relevant areas of linguistic theory would facilitate the efforts of those involved in different areas of professional writing. In particular, we feel that our understanding of the relationship between presupposition and tone would enable researchers to gain deeper insights, practitioners to write more effectively, instructors to teach more

Chapter 13: Conclusions

efficiently, and students to learn less painfully. (Riley and Parker, 1988: 341-342)

The most important thing to note about this conclusion is that it can be read straight through without the reader needing to stop at any point and go back into the paper to look for the definition of a term or for an illustration. This is because this conclusion is organized according to the paradigm: PROBLEM (paragraph 1)-APPROACH (first half of paragraph 2)-SOLUTION (second half of paragraph 2). Note, too, that the conclusion contains all of the elements found in an effective example: an ABSTRACTION (paragraphs 1 and 2), an ILLUSTRATION (paragraph 3), and an INTERPRETATION (paragraph 4).

Compare the previous passage to another conclusion, this one to a 14-page article entitled "Studying Writer-Reader Interactions in the Workplace."

Conclusion

>   This discussion aims to inspire researchers of writing in the workplace to expand their repertoire of research measures so they can capture more about how writers and readers interact. Already, a growing number of researchers are using process measures to observe writer-reader interactions in the workplace. It's exciting to envision the extent to which they and future researchers will broaden our knowledge about writing in the workplace, knowledge that, in turn, will help technical communication specialists develop broader theoretical perspectives and more informative writer-reader interaction models. Hopefully, these findings will filter down into classroom activities and assignments and will have a positive influence on technical writing students, preparing them better to handle the rhetorical complexities of their professions. (Spilka, 1988: 220-221)

Chapter 13: Conclusions

Given the title of the paper, the reader would expect to learn something about how writers and readers interact at work or how one should go about studying such interactions. Note, however, that this conclusion addresses neither of these issues. In fact, this conclusion contains no specific information at all. Instead, it focuses entirely on the author's personal response toward the topic of her article. (Note, for example, the use of the terms "inspire," "exciting," "envision," "future researchers," "hopefully," and so on.)

Another thing to keep in mind is that the longer and more complex the paper, the more self-contained the conclusion must be. For example, consider the following conclusion to a 20-page article by Parker, Riley, and Meyer entitled "Case Assignment and the Ordering of Constituents in Coordinate Structures." (Underlining has been added for ease of reference.)

Let us summarize our argument. First, we have tried to show that ordinary rules of case assignment in English are systematically suspended in coordinate constructions and that the explanation for this phenomenon is essentially structural. In particular, the NP dominating the coordinate structure blocks government and hence case assignment. Thus we get, for example, *Me and him left* alongside *He and I left*, but never **Me left* or **Him left*. Second, we have tried to show that the ordering of NP's within a coordinate construction is systematic, and that the system which determines ordering is essentially pragmatic. In particular, ordering is a function of the concept of empathy and is predicted by the interaction of a number of empathy hierarchies. Thus the Lexical Status Empathy Hierarchy correctly predicts, for example, the preference for *you and John* over *John and you*; the Person Empathy Hierarchy correctly predicts, for example, the preference for *you and him* over *him and you*; and the Case Empathy Hierarchy correctly predicts, for example, that *he and John* is more strongly preferred over *John and he* than *him and John* is over *John and him*.

Chapter 13: Conclusions

> The analysis presented in this paper indicates the continued relevance of current syntactic and pragmatic theory to the study of language variation. As we hope to have demonstrated, the use of unexpected case forms in coordinate constructions, a phenomenon typically associated with nonstandard varieties of English, is predictable from structural principles assumed in Chomsky's theories of government and barriers. Likewise, constituent ordering in both standard and nonstandard coordinate NP's is derivable from pragmatic principles assumed in Kuno's theory of empathy. (1988: 231)

Note especially the structure of the first paragraph, which is the actual summary. It consists of two points (designated by "First . . ." and "Second . . .") and each of these points is further broken down into a general point, followed by a particular point (designated by "In particular . . ."), followed by an illustration (designated by "for example . . .").

This rather longish paper on case assignment and coordinate structure was subsequently criticized by Graham Shorrocks, whom we eventually responded to. Now compare the conclusion of our original paper (above) to the conclusion of our much shorter response to Shorrocks (below). (Underlining has been added for ease of reference.)

> <u>In sum</u>, we do not object to constructive criticism, that is, criticism designed to elaborate and refine linguistic theory. Shorrocks' paper, however, doesn't meet this goal. <u>First</u>, his examples are not counter-evidence at all, but rather are actually *predicted* by Chomsky's theories of government and case assignment. <u>Second</u>, his inference that our claims must necessarily apply to any and all varieties of English throughout the world is simple peevishness. If our claims are restricted to his concept of "popular English," all of his objections disappear. <u>Third</u>, the existence of exceptions does not in and of itself countermand a theory, especially when that theory accounts in a simple way for a wide range of

Chapter 13: Conclusions

phenomena. The noted philosopher of science Thomas Kuhn points out that

> a theory must seem better than its competitors but it need not, and in fact never does, explain all the facts with which it can be confronted . . . . If any and every failure to fit were ground for theory rejection, all theories ought to be rejected at all times (1970, 17-18, 146).

(Parker, Riley, and Meyer, forthcoming)

Note that this conclusion still follows the format of a summary: "In sum . . ., First . . ., Second . . ., Third . . . ." However, it does not contain illustrations. This response is only six double-spaced pages (approximately three printed pages), and illustrations in the conclusion of such a short paper would be redundant.

One final note: although conclusions do not generally introduce anything *new*--no new concepts or illustrations not found in the body of the paper--they often do bring up related topics for future research. Consider the following conclusion to a short 5-page article entitled "Changes in Corporate Culture and Organizational Strategy: The Effect on Technical Writers." (Sentences have been numbered for ease of reference.)

Conclusion

(1) This paper identified two trends, high tech/high touch and greater worker participation, developing in the organizations in which our students will work. (2) It provided some interpretation of what those trends might mean to students as learners and us as teachers of technical writing. (3) Other trends are developing which still need to be considered. (4) For example, what might be the consequences on our technical writing students of working in

Chapter 13: Conclusions

>organizations which market their products worldwide? (5) Increasingly, organizations are entering the "global economy." (6) Should we be responding to that trend in our classrooms? (7) Being sensitive to trends and thinking about their consequences requires that in addition to our technical writing specialty, we stay current on a broad range of topics related to the organizations for which our students will write. (8) If we are serious about preparing our students for their most likely organizational future, we will need to be a step ahead. (Rawlins, 1988: 35)

Note that only the first two sentences summarize the topics covered in the paper. (Given the brevity of the article, it is unnecessary to go into much more detail.) The rest of the conclusion deals with questions for further research.

In short, the conclusion of a paper (like an abstract) must be self-contained. In fact, in journals that do not publish abstracts along with the article, the conclusion essentially serves as an abstract. (How many times have you picked up an article and flipped to the last page or two to get the gist of the piece?) Thus, it is important that your conclusion can be read straight through without the reader having to refer to the body of text. This becomes increasingly important as your paper becomes longer and more complex. As a microcosm of your argument and evidence, the conclusion should reflect the same PROBLEM-APPROACH-SOLUTION organization as your paper as a whole.

Chapter 14: Submitting Manuscripts For Publication

In previous chapters we have focused on ways to organize and develop research articles. Here we will turn our attention to the process of submitting a completed manuscript to a journal so that the editor can consider it for publication. As we'll see, although the submission process is not nearly so complex as the writing process, it nevertheless involves a number of decisions and, typically, a series of exchanges between you and the journal editor. In the sections below we will follow an article through some typical stages in the publication process.

Selecting a Journal

The time to begin thinking about where you will send an article is the day you first conceive of the idea. This is because, in any field, there are only a half-dozen or so good journals which would be interested in publishing any particular idea. By the time your article is finished, you should have three or four journals in mind that might be interested in publishing your paper. You certainly don't want to be in the position of writing an article that is of interest to only one single journal. If they reject it, you have no alternative. (The exception, of course, is the response article, which is typically of interest to only one journal.)

Chapter 14: Submitting Manuscripts for Publication

When you are ready to submit your manuscript for publication, you will need to select one of these journals as your first choice. This is because every journal that we know of has a policy (written or assumed) against multiple submissions, meaning that you cannot submit the same article to more than one journal simultaneously. This policy protects the editor from sending an article through the review process, only to have the author place it with another journal. At the same time, this can put the author at a disadvantage--especially in the humanities, where it often takes more than six months for an article to be accepted or rejected. Like it or not, however, multiple submissions are not considered ethical in most fields.

Our advice is to start at the top and work down. That is, send your paper to the best journal whose scope covers the topic of your paper. If the top journal rejects your article, then you can consider sending it to the next one on your list.

Before leaving the subject of journal selection, we want to say a few words about how to judge a journal's quality. As a rule, higher-quality journals exhibit several of the following traits:

- they are sponsored by a professional organization;
- they are published by a major university or by a national or international press;
- they have a "slick" appearance;
- they have been published for a relatively long period of time (i.e., 10 or more years);
- they are published on a regular basis, at least quarterly;
- they have a relatively high circulation, compared to other journals in the field;

Chapter 14: Submitting Manuscripts for Publication

- they publish articles that are cited frequently in other journals;
- their editorial board contains recognizable names in the field;
- they have a relatively high rejection rate.

Lower-quality journals, on the other hand, tend to lack many of these features. In short, select the highest-quality journal in which you can realistically expect to place your article.

Sending in the Manuscript

Most journals publish instructions for submitting manuscripts inside their front or back covers in every issue. Consider, for example, the following information taken from the inside back cover of the Spring 1994 issue of *American Speech*.

EDITORIAL POLICY

American Speech is concerned principally with the English language in the Western Hemisphere, although contributions dealing with English in other parts of the world, with other languages influencing English or influenced by it, and with general linguistic theory may also be submitted for consideration by the Editorial Board. The journal welcomes articles dealing with current usage, dialectology, and the history and structure of English. *American Speech* is not committed to any particular theoretical framework, but preference is given to articles that are likely to be of interest to a wide readership.

MANUSCRIPTS FOR PUBLICATION

Books for review and manuscripts of articles should be addressed to the editor, Ronald R. Butters, Department of English,

Chapter 14: Submitting Manuscripts for Publication

Duke University, Box 90018, Durham, NC 27708-0018. Studies of monograph length should be submitted to Publication of the American Dialect Society, edited by Allan Metcalf, Department of English, MacMurray College, Jacksonville, IL 62650. Send items for possible inclusion in "Among the New Words" to John Algeo, PO Box 270, Wheaton, IL 60189-0270.

Two copies of a manuscript should be submitted, and authors should retain a copy; manuscripts not accepted for publication will be returned if proper postage is included (loose stamps, please). Manuscripts should be prepared in conformity with the author-date system of *The MLA Style Manual* (1985, §5.7.1); for matters not discussed in *MLA*, consult the *Chicago Manual of Style*, 13th ed. Documentation must be given in the text itself with a list of references at the end. Endnotes should be on separate sheets, double-spaced, before the references list. Figures, tables, and graphic materials must be suitable for typesetting or photographic reproduction and should be placed on separate sheets at the end of the manuscript, with indication in the margin of the text at the place each is to be inserted.

Citation forms are to be italicized and glosses enclosed in single quotation marks, with intervening punctuation (e.g., *hushpuppy* `fried corn bread'). Technical terms and emphasized words should be indicated by double underlining for SMALL CAPITALS, rather than by italics. Phonetic and phonemic transcriptions should be restricted to the symbols of the International Phonetic Alphabet (IPA).

The information under "Editorial Policy" basically tells you what kind of subject matter the journal deals with: articles on the English language wherever it is spoken in the world, on English usage (e.g., *who* vs. *whom*) and dialectology, and on the history of the English language. Reading between the lines, you can infer that the journal does not publish articles which are primarily of a theoretical nature. Note that the statement says contributions dealing "with general linguistic theory may *also* be submitted" (emphasis added) and "preference is given to articles that are likely to be of interest to a wide readership."

Chapter 14: Submitting Manuscripts for Publication

This phraseology implies that the journal deals primarily with applied rather than theoretical linguistics.

Like most journals, this one gives authors specific guidelines for the manuscript's physical appearance and layout. The first paragraph under "Manuscripts for Publication" tells you who to send your paper to. (Note that different types of papers go to different people.) The second paragraph tells you how many copies to submit, which style sheet to use, and what format to follow for documentation, footnotes, and graphics. Finally, the third paragraph tells you how to use various typographical devices (e.g., italics, single quotes, small capitals, etc.).

Following such guidelines accomplishes two purposes. First, it helps you present your paper in a more favorable light; as one editor notes,

> A manuscript which does not conform to the journal's expectations for citations, headings, and style seems to come from an outsider rather than from a knowledgeable peer whose ideas are worth disseminating. . . . reviewers are more likely to recommend that a manuscript is worth revising if the author seems to come from the same discourse community . . . . An editor is more likely to ask an author to revise and resubmit a currently unacceptable manuscript when surface features suggest that the author will be able to revise the manuscript effectively. (Locker 1994: 64).

Second, following the submission guidelines will help the editor send your paper through the review process more quickly and efficiently. For example, many journals use a "blind" refereeing process, meaning that the editor does not tell the writer of an article the name of the reviewers, and doesn't

Chapter 14: Submitting Manuscripts for Publication

tell the reviewers of an article the name of its author. Consequently, these journals ask that any identifying information about the author (e.g., name, institution, etc.) appear only on the cover page of a manuscript (instead of, for example, at the top of each page). The editor of the *Journal of Business Communication* describes what happens when an author ignores this or other submission guidelines:

> Submitted papers that do not conform to the instructions create extra work for editors. For example, if an author sends me too few copies of a paper I could delay handling the paper until I can arrange for a student worker to make additional copies. But I usually want to speed the process along so I walk 87 steps--through five doors (two of which are usually locked) and down two flights of stairs--to the photocopier. Then I make the necessary copies and retrace my steps--this time *up* two flights of stairs--before continuing my work. The physical exercise is good for my heart, but I can think of better uses for my time. When a paper identifies the author or an institutional affiliation I white out the revealing words, make photocopies (as previously described) of the modified page, remove staples from the copies of the paper, insert the corrected page and re-staple. (Reinsch 1994: 59)

Given the relatively wide access to word-processing programs these days, there's really no excuse to submit a manuscript that *doesn't* adhere to a journal's guidelines. An hour or two at the keyboard is usually enough to re-format items like references, citation style, and so forth.

Speaking of word-processing, more and more journals are starting to accept manuscripts submitted on computer diskettes (along with a paper copy). Check the "Instructions to Authors" to see if the journal you're interested in accepts diskettes. If you can submit your article on a diskette that's compatible with the software used at the journal, you may speed

Chapter 14: Submitting Manuscripts for Publication

up the publication process and reduce the chance of errors when your article is typeset.

When you submit your paper, you will need a cover letter. You should use your institution's letterhead stationery and keep the content of the letter simple. Consider, for example, the following cover letter (on LSU stationery) used to submit an article co-authored by Parker and Kim Campbell.

May 19, 1992

Richard C. Gebhardt, Editor
College Composition and Communication
Department of English
Bowling Green State University
Bowling Green, OH 43403

Dear Professor Gebhardt:

We hope you will find the enclosed article, "Linguistics and Writing: A Reassessment," acceptable for publication in *College Composition and Communication.*

Sincerely,

Frank Parker
Professor

Note two things about the cover letter. First, it is simple. Don't try to explain your idea in the cover letter. The editor can find a synopsis of your paper by reading the abstract (if the journal requires one), the introduction, or the conclusion. Second, it includes the writer's rank. Indicate your rank if you are an assistant professor or higher. However, if you are a graduate student, don't mention this fact. There's no sense running the risk of prejudicing the editor or referees against you unnecessarily. If your paper is eventually accepted and the editor asks you for a short biographical statement about yourself, you can divulge your status at that point.

The Review Process

The editor of a reputable journal will generally acknowledge receipt of a manuscript, usually by postcard, within two or three weeks of receipt. (If you don't hear anything for a month, write the editor to inquire if the manuscript arrived.) Though most journals use a review process in which the editor sends your manuscript to two or more reviewers, there are times when an editor may reject your paper without sending it to reviewers. For example, the journal may have such a backlog of forthcoming articles that it is temporarily not accepting submissions. Or the editor may decide that your paper falls outside the scope of the journal's subject matter. More seriously, the editor may be certain that your paper would be rejected because of major flaws in its organization, methodology, or style.

Once the editor has made the decision to review your paper, he or she will send it to two or three referees. The refereeing process usually takes three to six months. (Many editors will tell you the estimated review time when they acknowledge receipt of your article.) If you don't get a decision on the paper within six months, write the editor to inquire about the status of the manuscript. The text of such a letter might read as follows:

Chapter 14: Submitting Manuscripts for Publication

> I am writing to inquire about an article, "Metadiscourse in Managerial Memos," which I submitted to your journal on March 14, 1994. At that time, you estimated that the review process would take three months. Since it has now been four months, I wanted to check on the article's status.
>
> Thank you for your help.

If you do not hear from the editor within a reasonable time (another month would be more than generous), then you should consider submitting your manuscript to another journal. If you decide to do this, you should inform the editor of the first journal with a brief letter stating "Since I have been unable to get a decision from you on my manuscript entitled '. . .,' I have decided to submit the paper to another journal."

In most cases, however, you will be kept informed. After receiving all of the referees' reports, the editor will write you with a decision. There are four basic decisions an editor can make on a manuscript: (1) ACCEPT WITHOUT CHANGE, (2) ACCEPT WITH MINOR REVISION, (3) REVISE AND RESUBMIT, and (4) REJECT. Decisions (1) and (4) are self-explanatory. Decision (2) means that the referees have minor objections to the paper's content and/or style, but the editor agrees to publish the paper if the authors make minor revisions and/or answer the referees' objections. Decision (3) means that the referees like the general idea expressed in the paper, but they have major objections to the paper's content and/or style and want to see a substantially revised version. The editor agrees to reconsider the paper (usually by sending it to the same referees) if the authors are willing to revise it.

The following letter was sent to Parker by the editor of *College Composition and Communication*.

Chapter 14: Submitting Manuscripts for Publication

> September 1, 1992
>
> Frank Parker and Kim Campbell
> c/o Frank Parker
> Department of English
> Louisiana State University
> Baton Rouge, LA 70803
>
> Dear Professor Parker:
>
> Thank you for sending "Linguistics and Writing: A Reassessment." I'm sorry not to have written earlier, but as I wrote you a couple weeks ago, your piece ran afoul of a Consulting Reader's schedule.
>
> I sent your essay to three Consulting Readers well-grounded in the subject. In their enclosed evaluations, they all support your project and two of them make suggestions and raise questions intended to strengthen the piece.
>
> My sense is that, with some work along lines suggested by Readers #2 and #3, your submission could work in *CCC*. And I look forward to seeing a new version which I would like to get reviewed by some or all of these Readers.
>
> Again, I'd like to thank you and Professor Campbell for supporting *CCC*.
>
> Sincerely,
>
> Richard C. Gebhardt, Editor

This letter is essentially a combination of decisions (2) and (3). The objections are minor, but the editor wants the referees to see the paper again before he makes the final decision to publish. What follows here are the exact reports from the three referees.

Chapter 14: Submitting Manuscripts for Publication

REFEREE #1

I like "Linguistics and Writing." It puts Crowley's article into perspective (too focused on pre 1980 linguistics and sentence-level studies) and shows how certain areas of linguistics--speech act theory, for instance--have indeed had some influence on contemporary writing instruction. I also like the way the authors, citing Riley, explain the relationship among theory, application, and practice. It's not exactly new stuff, but perhaps it's worth getting it into the general discussion about the value of linguistics or psychology or rhetoric in composition research and pedagogy. Perhaps differentiating theory from application and practice, as the authors do, helps explain, for instance, the reason we have difficulty explaining why sentence-combining works (Crowley's main complaint against it is that we don't know why it works). If SC is strictly practice, we would have to look at the theory behind it (linguistics) to find such answers. The differentiation might put other aspects of writing instruction into perspective as well.

REFEREE #2

CCC READER'S FORM

1. *FACTS, INTERPRETATIONS, CONCLUSIONS* ("How would you evaluate such things as the accuracy of information in the essay, the currency of the bibliography, the aptness of the author's interpretations, and the logic of the article's conclusions?")
In its facts, background, conclusions, etc., the submission is:
__ Very Strong √ Strong __ Adequate __ Weak __ Very Weak

2. *SCHOLARLY SIGNIFICANCE* ("How would you evaluate such things as the essay's originality, its significance for specialists in its field, and--if applicable--the quality of the research design? How likely is it that the article will be cited in future articles on the subject?")
In scholarly significance, the submission is:
__ Very Strong √ Strong __ Adequate __ Weak __ Very Weak

3. *PROFESSIONAL SIGNIFICANCE* ("How would you evaluate the significance this article might have for a diverse readership

Chapter 14: Submitting Manuscripts for Publication

including composition generalists, teachers looking for instructional ideas, and specialists in other areas?")
In broad professional significance, the submission is:
__ Very Strong √ Strong __ Adequate __ Weak __ Very Weak

4.   *CLARITY, READABILITY* ("How would you evaluate the essay's clarity? Did you find it hard to follow, fuzzy, obscure?")
In clarity and readability, the submission is:
√ Very Strong __ Strong __ Adequate __ Weak __ Very Weak

ADDITIONAL COMMENTS:

I found this essay very clearly written and organized. I agree with many of the authors' assumptions as well as many of their judgments about Crowley's essay. For me this piece shed light on some murky issues and raised some interesting questions. I think that it should sometime be published, but before it is, I think the authors would be wise to respond to the following questions:

1.   Could the authors state explicitly why they attach significance to the date 1965?

2.   Is it really fair to say that the structuralists did virtually no work on syntax (in the light of their immediate-constituent analysis and phrase-structure rules)?

3.   Shouldn't the authors mention more of the work such as that done by Teun A. van Dijk in textlinguistics?

4.   Is there any other work on defining disciplines and interdisciplines? Could we read about where this distinction came from or what it is related to?

5.   Wouldn't it be wise for the authors at the end to be more explicit about how the theories associated with the several examples really do move beyond sentence-level linguistics?

Chapter 14: Submitting Manuscripts for Publication

REFEREE #3

This piece provides a needed corrective to Crowley's somewhat reductive review, and its discussion of "disciplines" and "interdisciplines" should prove thought-provoking and controversial. I find the theory/application/practice distinctions fairly convincing (although I have a few reservations concerning the application/practice distinction), and I appreciate the numerous examples the authors provide to illustrate their classifications. I also suspect that a number of leaders in composition studies will want to challenge the authors' characterization of composition studies as an "interdiscipline" void of free-standing theory--but that's fine, because such reactions should stimulate a debate that could benefit the composition field. I'd recommend publishing this piece, and I see no need for extensive revision. However, I would recommend that the authors make a few minor adjustments.

Some suggestions, questions, and comments:

1. The repeated references to "post-1965 linguistics" will be clear to any linguists--they'll recognize 1965 as marking the publication of *Aspects* and the ascendancy of Standard Theory. However, some (most?) *CCC* readers will not recognize the significance of this date. I'd recommend adding a footnote explaining its significance (and possibly directing readers to Newmeyer's *Linguistic Theory in America* for a more detailed explanation).

2. At the top of page 7 the authors note, "It is generally recognized that composition has been in a state of theoretical turmoil for some time." I'd recommend changing this to "Only recently has composition studies shown signs of emerging from a state of theoretical turmoil." Such a change would, I think, more accurately reflect Hairston's intentions in the "Winds of Change" piece (mentioned in footnote 9).

However, regardless of whether the authors make this change, footnote 9 should cite at least one recent source--if they base their generalization on two 1983 sources, they invite the same sort of criticism that they're leveling at Crowley. (In fact, the second paragraph on page 7 *does* cite a recent source--North's book. Maybe North should be mentioned along with Hairston and Connors in the

Chapter 14: Submitting Manuscripts for Publication

note?) If the authors are looking for another recent source to cite concerning theoretical turmoil in composition, they might consider Linda Flower's "Cognition, Context, and Theory Building" (*CCC* 40 [Oct. 1989] 282-311)--a piece that acknowledges the need for composition studies to resolve the dispute between its cognitivist and social-constructionist factions.

A point to ponder: it seems to me that the current theoretical dispute between composition's cognitivists and social constructionists is different in kind from the turmoil that raged two decades ago. The current dispute seems (to me anyway) a local skirmish similar to those that occur regularly in linguistics (e.g., the dispute throughout the 1970s between the generative semanticists and the Chomskyan faction or the more recent dispute between GB advocates and the generalized phrase structure proponents). In contrast, the earlier composition disputes (to which Hairston and Connors allude) signaled a paradigmatic shift comparable to that in linguistics from structuralism to generativism. In brief, I'm suggesting that the authors may have overestimated the extent to which composition currently is in a state of "theoretical turmoil." I wouldn't require them to revise their stance as a condition for publishing this piece, but I do think they could avoid some criticism with some judicious rephrasing.

3. I suspect that the few compositionists who borrow from linguistics are most likely to borrow from text linguists such as van Dijk (or possibly from psycholinguists such as Schank). While I don't see it as essential that the authors mention text linguistics--their piece makes its point nicely without broaching this area--I do wonder how they view text linguistics. What is its relationship to linguistics proper? Is it a discipline or an interdiscipline? Maybe this is a topic for another paper.

4. Note 11 does illustrate a point; however, the reference to *CCC's* associate editor might raise questions concerning the journal's impartiality in handling this article. Maybe the authors should delete this note.

5. The authors will need to convert the Works Cited entries to MLA format (adding first names for authors, etc.).

Chapter 14: Submitting Manuscripts for Publication

There are three things to note about these referees' reports. First, they differ considerably in the amount of feedback that they give the authors--they range from a short paragraph in the first report to two single-spaced pages in the third. Second, the first raises no objections, whereas the second and third do. Moreover, where the second report raises objections, the third raises objections *and* tells the authors how to answer them. Thus, the third report is the most useful for purposes of revision. Third, two of the reports (the second and third) raise two of the same questions: the significance of the year 1965 and the status of van Dijk's text linguistics. This is significant. When one referee raises an objection, it may be simply an idiosyncrasy of the reviewer; however, when two or more referees make the same criticism, the authors simply *must* deal with it.

After spending four weeks thinking about the referees' reports and consulting long-distance with each other, Parker and Campbell revised the paper and sent it to the editor with the following cover letter.

Chapter 14: Submitting Manuscripts for Publication

September 27, 1992

Richard C. Gebhardt, Editor
<u>College Composition and Communication</u>
Bowling Green State University
Bowling Green, OH 43403

Dear Professor Gebhardt:

Thank you for your letter of September 1. Kim Campbell and I have revised "Linguistics and Writing: A Reassessment" along the lines suggested by your readers. Specifically, we have addressed the following issues.

1. We changed the sentence on the top of page 7, as suggested by the third reader.
2. We added a paragraph on page 21 supporting the claim that our examples move beyond sentence-level linguistics.
3. We added footnote 2 explaining the significance of the year 1965.
4. We added footnote 8 explaining the origin of immediate constituent analysis and its relation to phrase structure grammars.
5. We added more recent references to footnote 11, as suggested by the third reader.
6. We added footnote 13 explaining the relation of text linguistics to our discussion.
7. We deleted the footnote about <u>CCC</u>'s associate editor, as suggested by the third reader.
8. We added authors' first names to the Works Cited.

We want to say that we found your readers' comments <u>extremely</u> useful. The third reader, in particular, told us not only what was wrong but also how to fix it. <u>CCC</u> is lucky to have readers like these.

We hope that your readers will find these changes satisfactory; however, we will be more than happy to consider any other changes they think are necessary.

Sincerely,

Frank Parker
Professor

Chapter 14: Submitting Manuscripts for Publication

There are several things to note about the authors' response to the reviewers in this case. First, the authors revised the manuscript and returned it to the editor within a month. Let's face it, there's nothing more frustrating than going back and revising a piece of writing you thought was finished. However, when a journal asks for revisions, it's crucially important to get the revisions to them as soon as you can. If you wait too long, the editorship may change hands and the new editor could refuse to honor his or her predecessor's commitments. Also, after a long wait, you can lose interest in the paper and simply forget your chain of reasoning. In addition, if the editor wants the referees to review the revised manuscript, it's to your advantage for the referees to have your work fresh in *their* minds. Don't tarry--this is clearly a case of a "bird in the hand."

Second, note that the authors list their revisions in point form and explain the relevance of each change. This not only makes the revisions easy for the editor and the referees to find, but it also shows that the authors took the referees' comments seriously.

Third, the authors express a willingness to make further changes if necessary. This keeps the lines of communication open, just in case one of the referees is not completely satisfied with these revisions.

About two months after submitting the revised manuscript, the authors got the final decision from the editor that the manuscript had been accepted for publication. Along with the letter of acceptance came a contract, which is fairly typical of the ones authors of journal articles are asked to sign. We've reproduced a copy of the actual contract here.

Chapter 14: Submitting Manuscripts for Publication

College Composition and Communication

College Composition and Communication

The Conference on College Composition and Communication of the National Council of Teachers of English is pleased to inform you of its intention to publish your contribution to *College Composition and Communication (CCC)* entitled

LINGUISTICS AND WRITING: A REASSESSMENT

The intent to publish is, of course, contingent upon the journal office receiving mutually acceptable final copy according to the scheduled deadlines and in conformity with house style and usage, and upon the timely return of a signed copy of this consent to publish form. Final decision about if and when to publish your contribution rests with the *College Composition and Communication* Editor.

Consent to Publish — Whereas the National Council of Teachers of English (hereafter NCTE) undertakes to publish *CCC*, of which the undersigned is Author of one or more parts, the Author grants and assigns exclusively to NCTE for its use any and all rights of whatsoever kind or nature now or hereafter protected by the Copyright Laws (common or statutory) of the United States and all foreign countries in all languages in and to the above-named article, including all subsidiary rights. NCTE, in turn, grants to the Author the rights of republication in any book of which he or she is the author or editor, subject only to the granting of proper credits in the book to the original publication of the article by NCTE in *CCC*.

Previous Publication — The Author guarantees that the article furnished for *CCC* has not been previously published elsewhere and, to the best of his or her knowledge, is original. Otherwise, for anything that has been previously published elsewhere, in whole or in part, permission has been obtained by the author for publication in *CCC* using applicable NCTE release form or equivalent, and the Author will submit with the manuscript the exact wording of credit lines for such permission, along with originals of signed release forms.

Subsidiary Rights Compensation — Should NCTE receive a request to reprint or translate all or any portion of the author's article for commercial use, NCTE will attempt to obtain the author's approval for the requested use (excluding fair use). This attempt shall include a letter sent to the last known address of the author outlining the use, proposed fee*, if any, and allowing 30 days for a response. Failure to respond in the stated time period will constitute consent. Fees will be handled according to the NCTE Permissions Policy.

If the foregoing terms are satisfactory please sign and date this agreement. Immediately return one copy to *CCC* and retain the other copy for your files.

Editor _____ Date November 24, 1992

Author Richard C. Gebhardt _____ Date _____

*See NCTE Permissions Policy enclosed.

National Council of Teachers of English

Richard C. Gebhardt, Editor
Department of English
(419) 372-6839

Bowling Green State University
Bowling Green, Ohio 43403

Chapter 14: Submitting Manuscripts for Publication

The first paragraph basically gives the publisher the right to edit the paper for style and to determine what issue of the journal it appears in.

The paragraph labeled "Consent to Publish" transfers the copyright from the authors to the publisher, but it also retains for the authors the right to re-publish all or any part of the same article in any other work of their creation. This is a very important clause in any publishing contract. You always want to be able to re-use any intellectual material of your creation. (Incidentally, this is the reason that we have used so much of our own previously published material for examples in this book. We have retained the right to reproduce our own work; but we have to get permission to reproduce the work of others, which can be time-consuming and costly.)

The paragraph labeled "Previous Publication" basically makes the authors (and not the publisher) responsible if the article contains any uncredited material owned by a third party. The rest of this contract is pretty much self-explanatory.

As you can see, the entire review process for this article took just over six months--from May 19, 1992, when the article was first submitted, to November 26, 1992, when the final decision to publish was made.

After Your Article Is Accepted

After your article has been accepted, your only other task is to read and correct the proofs. How quickly you get these will vary from field to field and from journal to journal; they may arrive anywhere from a few months to a year after

Chapter 14: Submitting Manuscripts for Publication

acceptance. When reading proofs, there are three principles to keep in mind.

First, have someone help you. Ideally, a friend should read aloud to you from your original manuscript, while you read the proofs silently and mark any necessary corrections. If you read only the proofs without referring to the original manuscript, you won't be able to tell if an entire sentence--or perhaps even an entire paragraph--has accidentally been omitted. And it's nearly impossible to compare the original to the proofs by trying to read both of them yourself. (Incidentally, we like to make a copy of the proofs before going through the reading stage. That way, the proofreader can mark the copy during the reading stage, then transfer the corrections neatly onto the copy that goes back to the editor.)

Second, when marking the proofs, use the proofreader's symbols provided by the editor. If none are provided, you can find a list of standard proofreader's symbols in most hardcover dictionaries or style manuals. Keep in mind that the changes you make must be interpreted by a printer, not by someone who is familiar with the terminology and subject matter of your field. This means that your marks must be clear and consistent with the conventions of the printing profession. If you're completely unfamiliar with proofreader's symbols, make sure you clearly spell out your corrections in the margins (e.g., "Insert semicolon between *event* and *however*").

Third, return the proofs promptly. Aim to get them back in the mail within a week after you receive them. The reasons for this should be self-evident: the faster you return your proofs, the faster your article can go to press.

Chapter 14: Submitting Manuscripts for Publication

We should note that the proofreading stage is *not* the time to make revisions. Naturally you can re-insert any material that was accidentally omitted from your manuscript when it was being typeset. However, you cannot decide to re-phrase sentences, rearrange paragraphs, or add new material at this point. Any such changes that you make at the proof stage will have a domino effect on the layout of your article and may affect the pagination and layout of other articles in the same issue. For this reason, many journals charge you a stiff fee for making substantive changes in proofs. Therefore, resist the urge to tighten or embellish your style at this point--live with the article that you originally wrote.

After your article finally sees print--typically a few months after you have returned the proofs--you will receive either some copies of the issue in which it appears or a set of offprints (copies of just your article). Offprints are a handy way to distribute your work to interested parties--your department head, prospective employers, and other colleagues.

In this chapter we've gone through the process of submitting a manuscript from start to finish. As you can see, this process can be tedious; it requires a lot of patience and attention to detail. The payoff, however, is worth the effort. Remember: every faculty member at every university teaches and serves on committees, but only some of them publish.

Chapter 15: Conclusion

It should be obvious that there is much more to producing publishable academic writing than what we have been able to cover in this one short book. At the same time, however, we believe that a novice can at least *begin* to write for academic publication within the space of one or two semesters. We have seen graduate students do this repeatedly over the last 15 years. The key to accomplishing this rests on five fundamental principles.

1. Start now. The minute you are faced with an assignment, your mind goes to work on it (at least unconsciously). Take advantage of this fact--an hour or two every day spent on a project is easier and more productive than trying to cram three months of work into a week. Most successful writers will tell you they never work more than a few hours a day.

2. Be considerate. Never assume your audience will be able (or willing) to make sense out of something that you yourself find confusing or boring. Consideration for your reader, however, requires work. In a recent interview on National Public Radio, Fran Lebowitz was asked if writing was difficult for her. She responded that it was, but added that "You should make it harder on yourself to write, so that you're easier to read."

3. Less is more. As students, we are all led to substitute long writing for good writing; however, don't indulge in this practice. Heed the words of Blaise Pascal, who once

Chapter 15: Conclusion

wrote to a friend, "I have made this letter longer than usual, because I lack the time to make it short" (*Lettres Provinciales*).

4. Assume the worst. Your all-forgiving mother *may* try to read your article, but it should be worded and documented to withstand the scrutiny of the most unsympathetic reader. Your readers may not agree with what you write, but they should never be able to dismantle your argument.

5. Be self-assured. Don't be intimidated by the idea of competing for journal space with Ph.D.'s who have years of experience. The fact is that beginners are subject to insights unavailable to older practitioners. Philosopher of science Thomas Kuhn notes that "almost always [those] who achieve [the] fundamental inventions of a new paradigm have been either very young or very new to the field" (1970: 90).

Good luck!

References

Campbell, Kim S. "Structural Cohesion in Technical Texts." *Journal of Technical Writing and Communication* 21 (1991): 221-37.

_____, Kathryn Riley, and Frank Parker. "*You*-Perspective: More Insights from Speech Act Theory." *Journal of Technical Writing and Communication* 20 (1990): 189-99.

Day, Robert A. *How to Write and Publish a Scientific Paper.* Philadelphia: ISI Press, 1983.

Ferguson, K. Scott, and Frank Parker. "Grammar and Technical Writing." *Journal of Technical Writing and Communication* 20 (1990): 357-67.

Fesmire, Alice A. Review of *Not Only English: Affirming America's Multilingual Heritage* edited by H. A. Daniels. *Journal of Technical Writing and Communication* 22 (1992): 223-26.

Flower, Linda, John R. Hayes, Linda Carey, Karen Schriver, and James Stratman. "Detection, Diagnosis, and the Strategies of Revision." *College Composition and Communication* 37 (1986): 16-55.

Fox, Cynthia A. "New England French in New York State: The French of Cohoes, New York." *Newsletter of the American Dialect Society* 23.3 (1991): 5.

References

Gebhardt, Richard. "Scholarship, Promotion, and Tenure in Composition Studies." *College Composition and Communication* 44 (1993): 439-42.

Graff, Bennett. Letter to the editor. *MLA Newsletter* 26 (Fall 1994): 12-13.

Harris, R. Allen. "Linguistics, Technical Writing, and Generalized Phrase Structure Grammar." *Journal of Technical Writing and Communication* 18 (1988): 227-240.

_____. "Commentary: A Response to K. Scott Ferguson and Frank Parker's 'Grammar and Technical Writing.'" *Journal of Technical Writing and Communication* 22 (1992): 53-56.

Kuhn, Thomas. *The Structure of Scientific Revolutions*, 2nd ed. Chicago: U of Chicago Press, 1970.

Larson, Richard. Quoted in "Freshman Composition: Is it a Waste of Time?" *The Council Chronicle* (April 1992): 9.

LeComte, Edward. Forum. *PMLA* 109 (1994): 443.

Limaye, Mohan, and David A. Victor. "Cross-Cultural Business Communication Research: State of the Art and Hypotheses for the 1990's." *Journal of Business Communication* 28 (1991): 277-95.

Locker, Kitty. "Turning a Presentation into an Article." *The Bulletin of the Association for Business Communication* 57 (1994): 63-65.

References

Lovejoy, Kim B. "The Gricean Model: A Revising Rubric." *Journal of Teaching Writing* 6 (1987): 9-18.

Manning, Alan. "Literary vs. Technical Writing: Substitutes vs. Standards for Reality." *Journal of Technical Writing and Communication* 18 (1988): 241-62.

――――. "Abstracts in Relation to Larger and Smaller Discourse Structures." *Journal of Technical Writing and Communication* 20 (1990): 369-90.

――――. Review of *English Grammar: Principles and Facts* by J. Kaplan. *ADS Teaching Newsletter* (1993): 3-4. In *Newsletter of the American Dialect Society* 25.3 (1993).

Mulcahy, Patricia. "Writing Reader-Based Instructions: Strategies to Build Coherence." *The Technical Writing Teacher* 15 (1988): 234-43.

Parker, Frank. Review of *Language Typology 1985: Papers from the Linguistic Typology Symposium, Moscow, 9-13 December 1985* edited by W. P. Lehmann. *South Central Review* (1988): 117-19.

――――, and Kim S. Campbell. "Linguistics and Writing: A Reassessment." *College Composition and Communication* 44 (1993): 295-314.

――――, Kathryn Riley, and Charles Meyer. "Case Assignment and the Ordering of Constituents in Coordinate Constructions." *American Speech* 63 (1988): 214-33.

Popken, Randall. "A Study of Topic Sentence Use in Technical Writing." *The Technical Writing Teacher* 18 (1991): 49-58.

References

Rawlins, Claudia. "Changes in Corporate Culture and Organizational Strategy: The Effect on Technical Writers." *The Technical Writing Teacher* 15 (1988): 31-35.

Reinsch, N. L. "Some Gentle Reminders." *The Bulletin of the Association for Business Communication* 57 (1994): 59-61.

Riley, Kathryn. "Pragmatics and Technical Writing: Some Further Considerations." *The Technical Writing Teacher* 13 (1986): 160-70.

―――――. "Speech Act Theory and Degrees of Directness in Professional Writing." *The Technical Writing Teacher* 15 (1988a): 1-29.

―――――. "Conversational Implicature and Unstated Meaning in Professional Communication." *The Technical Writing Teacher* 15 (1988b): 94-104.

―――――. "Passive Voice and Rhetorical Role in Scientific Writing." *Journal of Technical Writing and Communication* 21 (1991): 239-57.

―――――. Review of *English Grammar: Principles and Facts* by J. Kaplan. *Language* (1991): 867-68.

―――――, and Frank Parker. "Tone as a Function of Presupposition in Technical and Business Writing." *Journal of Technical Writing and Communication* 18 (1988): 325-43.

Saha, P. K. "Reflexives Revisited." *American Speech* 68.3 (1993): 319-20.

References

Smeltzer, Larry, and Gail Thomas. "Managers as Writers." *Journal of Business and Technical Communication* 8 (1994): 186-211.

Spilka, Rachel. "Studying Writer-Reader Interactions in the Workplace." *The Technical Writing Teacher* 15 (1988): 208-21.

Thomason, Sarah G. "The Editor's Department." *Language* (1990): 659.

Thompson, Isabelle. "The Given/New Contract and Cohesion: Some Suggestions for Classroom Practice." *Journal of Technical Writing and Communication* 15 (1985): 205-14.

Underwood, Gary N. Review of *Language Variety in the South: Perspectives in Black and White* edited by M. Montgomery and G. Bailey. *South Atlantic Review* (1988): 142-45.

Vande Kopple, William J. "Themes, Thematic Progression, and Some Implications for Understanding Discourse." *Written Communication* 8 (1991): 311-47.

Zhang, Zaixin. "Ranking of Indirectness in Professional Writing." *Journal of Technical Writing and Communication* 20 (1990): 291-305.